ALL NEW
SLOW
COOKER

Contents

In the Beginning

Chicken Wings in Honey Sauce (page 4)

Chicken Wings in Honey Sauce

    3 pounds chicken wings (16 wings)
      Salt and black pepper to taste
    2 cups honey
    1 cup soy sauce
    ½ cup ketchup
    ¼ cup oil
    2 cloves garlic, minced
      Sesame seeds (optional)

SLOW COOKER DIRECTIONS

Rinse chicken and pat dry with paper towels. Cut off and discard wing tips. Cut each wing at joint to make two sections. Sprinkle wings with salt and pepper. Place wings on broiler pan. Broil 4 to 5 inches from heat 20 minutes, 10 minutes a side or until chicken is brown. Transfer chicken to CROCK-POT® Slow Cooker.

For sauce, combine honey, soy sauce, ketchup, oil and garlic in bowl. Pour over chicken wings. Cover and cook on Low 4 to 5 hours or on High 2 to 2½ hours. Garnish with sesame seeds, if desired.

Makes about 32 appetizers

Hot Mulled Cider

    ½ gallon apple cider
    ½ cup packed light brown sugar
    1½ teaspoons balsamic or cider vinegar
    1 teaspoon vanilla
    1 cinnamon stick
    6 whole cloves
    ½ cup applejack or bourbon (optional)

Combine all ingredients in slow cooker. Cover and cook on LOW 5 to 6 hours. Discard cinnamon stick and cloves. Serve in hot mugs.

Makes 16 servings

Party Mix

3 cups bite-sized rice cereal
2 cups O-shaped oat cereal
2 cups bite-sized shredded wheat cereal
1 cup peanuts, pecans or cashews
1 cup thin pretzel sticks (optional)
½ cup butter or margarine, melted
4 tablespoons Worcestershire sauce
  Dash hot pepper sauce
½ teaspoon seasoned salt
½ teaspoon garlic salt
½ teaspoon onion salt

SLOW COOKER DIRECTIONS
Combine cereals, nuts and pretzels in CROCK-POT® Slow Cooker. Mix melted butter with remaining ingredients in small bowl; pour over cereal mixture in CROCK-POT® Slow Cooker and toss lightly to coat. *Do not cover CROCK-POT® Slow Cooker.* Cook on High 2 hours, stirring well every 30 minutes; turn to Low for 2 to 6 hours. Store in airtight container. *Makes 10 cups mix*

Spiced Apple Tea

  3 bags cinnamon herbal tea
  3 cups boiling water
  2 cups unsweetened apple juice
  6 whole cloves
  1 cinnamon stick

Place tea bags in slow cooker. Pour boiling water over tea bags; cover and let stand 10 minutes. Remove and discard tea bags. Add apple juice, cloves and cinnamon stick to slow cooker. Cover and cook on LOW 2 to 3 hours. Remove and discard cloves and cinnamon stick. Serve in warm mugs.   *Makes 4 servings*

Viennese Coffee

  3 cups strong freshly brewed hot coffee
  3 tablespoons chocolate syrup
  1 teaspoon sugar
  ⅓ cup heavy cream
  ¼ cup crème de cacao or Irish cream (optional)
    Whipped cream
    Chocolate shavings for garnish

Combine coffee, chocolate syrup and sugar in slow cooker. Cover and cook on LOW 2 to 2½ hours. Stir in heavy cream and crème de cacao, if using. Cover and cook 30 minutes or until heated through.

Ladle coffee into coffee cups; top with whipped cream and chocolate shavings.   *Makes about 4 servings*

Viennese Coffee

Easiest Three-Cheese Fondue

1 tablespoon margarine
¼ cup finely chopped onion
2 cloves garlic, minced
1 tablespoon all-purpose flour
¾ cup reduced-fat (2%) milk
2 cups (8 ounces) shredded mild or sharp Cheddar cheese
1 package (3 ounces) cream cheese, cut into cubes
½ cup (2 ounces) crumbled blue cheese
⅛ teaspoon ground red pepper
4 to 6 drops hot pepper sauce
    Assorted fresh vegetables or breadsticks for dipping

Combine all ingredients *except* fresh vegetables in slow cooker. Cover and cook on LOW 2 to 2½ hours, stirring once or twice, until cheese is melted and smooth. Increase heat to HIGH and cook 1 to 1½ hours or until heated through. Serve with fresh vegetables or breadsticks.
Makes 8 (3-tablespoon) servings

Hint: For a special touch, sprinkle fondue with parsley and ground red pepper.

Lighten Up: To reduce the total fat, replace the Cheddar cheese and cream cheese with reduced-fat Cheddar and cream cheeses.

Turkey Meatballs in Cranberry-Barbecue Sauce

1 can (16 ounces) jellied cranberry sauce
½ cup barbecue sauce
1 egg white
1 pound ground turkey
1 green onion with top, sliced
2 teaspoons grated orange peel
1 teaspoon reduced-sodium soy sauce
¼ teaspoon black pepper
⅛ teaspoon ground red pepper (optional)

Combine cranberry sauce and barbecue sauce in slow cooker. Cover and cook on HIGH 20 to 30 minutes or until cranberry sauce is melted and mixture is hot, stirring every 10 minutes.

Meanwhile, place egg white in medium bowl; beat lightly. Add turkey, green onion, orange peel, soy sauce, black pepper and ground red pepper, if desired; mix well with hands until well blended. Shape into 24 balls.

Spray large nonstick skillet with nonstick cooking spray. Add meatballs to skillet; cook over medium heat 8 to 10 minutes or until meatballs are no longer pink in center, carefully turning occasionally to brown evenly. Add to heated sauce in slow cooker; stir gently to coat evenly with sauce.

Reduce heat to LOW. Cover and cook 3 hours. When ready to serve, transfer meatballs to serving plate; garnish, if desired. Serve with decorative picks. *Makes 12 servings*

Turkey Meatballs in Cranberry-Barbecue Sauce

Steaming Chilis

Southwest Bean Chili (page 14)

Southwest Bean Chili

1 can (15 ounces) garbanzo beans, rinsed and drained
1 can (15 ounces) red kidney beans, rinsed and drained
1 can (15 ounces) black beans, rinsed and drained
1 cup chicken broth
4 cloves garlic, minced
1½ cups frozen corn
2 medium green bell peppers, seeded and chopped
1 can (16 ounces) tomato sauce
1 can (14½ ounces) Mexican-style stewed tomatoes, undrained
3 tablespoons chili powder
1 tablespoon cocoa powder
1 teaspoon ground cumin
½ teaspoon salt
  Hot cooked rice
  Shredded cheese, ripe olives, avocado and green onion slices
  (optional)

Combine all ingredients *except* rice and toppings in slow cooker. Cover and cook on LOW 6 to 6½ hours or until vegetables are tender.

Spoon rice into bowls; top with chili. Serve with shredded cheese, ripe olives, avocado and green onion slices, if desired.

Makes 8 to 10 servings

Chili Verde

¾ pound boneless lean pork, cut into 1-inch cubes
1 large onion, halved and thinly sliced
6 cloves garlic, chopped or sliced
1 pound fresh tomatillos, coarsely chopped
1 can (about 14 ounces) chicken broth
1 can (4 ounces) diced mild green chilies
1 teaspoon ground cumin
1 can (15 ounces) Great Northern beans, rinsed and drained
½ cup lightly packed fresh cilantro, chopped
  Sour cream

Spray large skillet with nonstick cooking spray and heat over medium-high heat. Add pork; cook until browned on all sides.

Combine cooked pork and all remaining ingredients *except* cilantro and sour cream in slow cooker. Cover and cook on HIGH 3 to 4 hours. Season to taste with salt and pepper. Gently press meat against side of slow cooker with wooden spoon to shred. Reduce heat to LOW. Stir in cilantro and cook 10 minutes. Serve with sour cream.

Makes 4 servings

White Bean Chili

       1 pound ground chicken
       3 cups coarsely chopped celery
       1 can (16 ounces) whole tomatoes, undrained and coarsely
           chopped
       1 can (15½ ounces) Great Northern beans, drained and rinsed
    1½ cups coarsely chopped onions
       1 cup chicken broth
       4 teaspoons chili powder
       3 cloves garlic, minced
    1½ teaspoons ground cumin
     ¾ teaspoon ground allspice
     ¾ teaspoon ground cinnamon
     ½ teaspoon pepper

Spray large nonstick skillet with cooking spray; heat over high heat until hot. Add chicken; cook until browned, breaking into pieces with fork. Add remaining ingredients to slow cooker; stir well. Cover and cook on LOW 5½ to 6 hours or until chicken is no longer pink and celery is tender.

Makes 6 servings

Chunky Vegetable Chili

2 cans (about 15 ounces *each*) Great Northern beans, rinsed and
   drained
1 cup frozen corn
1 medium onion, chopped
2 ribs celery, diced
1 can (6 ounces) tomato paste
1 can (4 ounces) diced mild green chilies, undrained
1 carrot, diced
3 cloves garlic, minced
1 tablespoon chili powder
2 teaspoons dried oregano leaves
1 teaspoon salt
1 cup water
   Assorted crackers

Combine beans, corn, onion, celery, tomato paste, green chilies, carrot,
garlic, chili powder, oregano and salt in slow cooker. Stir in water.
Cover and cook on LOW 5½ to 6 hours or until vegetables are tender.
Serve with assorted crackers.   *Makes 6 servings*

Turkey Vegetable Chili Mac

¾ pound ground turkey breast
 1 can (about 15 ounces) black beans, rinsed and drained
 1 can (14½ ounces) Mexican-style stewed tomatoes, undrained
 1 can (14½ ounces) no-salt-added diced tomatoes, undrained
 1 cup frozen corn
½ cup chopped onion
 2 cloves garlic, minced
 1 teaspoon Mexican seasoning
½ cup uncooked elbow macaroni
⅓ cup sour cream

Spray large skillet with nonstick cooking spray. Add turkey; cook until browned. Combine cooked turkey, beans, tomatoes, corn, onion, garlic and seasoning in slow cooker. Cover and cook on LOW 4 to 5 hours.

Stir in macaroni. Cover and cook 10 minutes; stir. Cover and cook 20 to 30 minutes or until pasta is tender. Serve with sour cream.

Makes 6 servings

Turkey Vegetable Chili Mac

Chunky Chili

    1 pound lean ground beef
    1 medium onion, chopped
    1 tablespoon chili powder
  1½ teaspoons ground cumin
    2 cans (16 ounces *each*) diced tomatoes, undrained
    1 can (15 ounces) pinto beans, rinsed and drained
    ½ cup prepared salsa
      Salt and pepper
    ½ cup (2 ounces) shredded Cheddar cheese
    3 tablespoons sour cream
    4 teaspoons sliced black olives

Heat large skillet over medium heat. Add beef and onion; cook until beef is browned and onion is tender. Drain fat. Place beef mixture, chili powder, cumin, tomatoes, beans and salsa in slow cooker; stir. Cover and cook on LOW 5 to 6 hours or until flavors are blended and chili is bubbly. Season with salt and pepper to taste. Serve with cheese, sour cream and olives.   *Makes 4 (1½-cup) servings*

Serving Suggestion: Serve with tossed green salad and cornbread muffins.

Black and White Chili

    1 pound chicken tenders, cut into ¾-inch pieces
    1 cup coarsely chopped onion
    1 can (15½ ounces) Great Northern beans, drained
    1 can (15 ounces) black beans, drained
    1 can (14½ ounces) Mexican-style stewed tomatoes, undrained
    2 tablespoons Texas-style chili powder seasoning mix

Spray large saucepan with nonstick cooking spray; heat over medium heat until hot. Add chicken and onion; cook and stir 5 minutes or until chicken is browned.

Combine cooked chicken, onion, beans, tomatoes and chili seasoning in slow cooker. Cover and cook on LOW 4 to 4½ hours.
Makes 6 (1-cup) servings

Chunky Chili

Soups & Stews

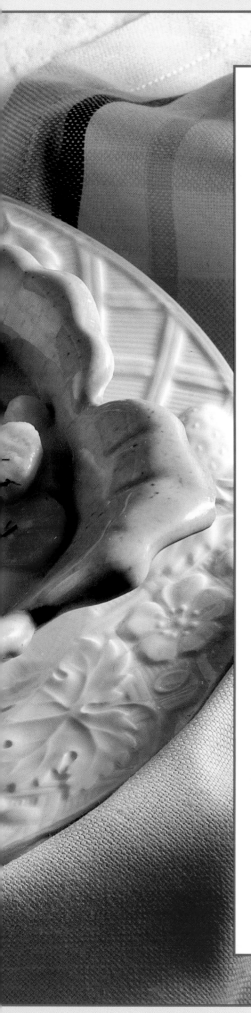

Country Chicken Chowder (page 24)

Country Chicken Chowder

    2 tablespoons margarine or butter
 1½ pounds chicken tenders, cut into ½-inch pieces
    2 small onions, chopped
    2 ribs celery, sliced
    2 small carrots, sliced
    2 cups frozen corn
    2 cans (10¾ ounces *each*) cream of potato soup
 1½ cups chicken broth
    1 teaspoon dried dill weed
    ½ cup half-and-half

Melt margarine in large skillet. Add chicken; cook until browned. Add cooked chicken, onions, celery, carrots, corn, soup, chicken broth and dill to slow cooker. Cover and cook on LOW 3 to 4 hours or until chicken is no longer pink and vegetables are tender.

Turn off heat; stir in half-and-half. Cover and let stand 5 to 10 minutes or just until heated through.   *Makes 8 servings*

Note: For a special touch, garnish soup with croutons and fresh dill.

Hearty Cassoulet

    1 tablespoon olive oil
    1 large onion, finely chopped
    4 boneless skinless chicken thighs (about 1 pound), chopped
    ¼ pound smoked turkey sausage, finely chopped
    3 cloves garlic, minced
    1 teaspoon dried thyme leaves
    ½ teaspoon ground black pepper
    4 tablespoons tomato paste
    2 tablespoons water
    3 cans (about 15 ounces *each*) Great Northern beans, rinsed and
       drained
    ½ cup dry bread crumbs
    3 tablespoons minced fresh parsley

Heat oil in large skillet over medium heat until hot. Add onion; cook and stir 5 minutes or until onion is tender. Stir in chicken, sausage, garlic, thyme and black pepper. Cook 5 minutes or until chicken and sausage are browned.

Remove skillet from heat; stir in tomato paste and water until blended. Place beans and chicken mixture in slow cooker; cover and cook on LOW 4 to 4½ hours. Just before serving, combine bread crumbs and parsley in small bowl. Sprinkle on top of cassoulet. *Makes 6 servings*

French-Style Pork Stew

```
 1 tablespoon vegetable oil
 1 pork tenderloin (16 ounces), cut into ¾- to 1-inch cubes
 1 medium onion, coarsely chopped
 1 rib celery, sliced
 ½ teaspoon dried basil leaves
 ¼ teaspoon dried rosemary leaves, crushed
 ¼ teaspoon dried oregano leaves
 2 tablespoons all-purpose flour
 1 cup chicken broth
 ½ package (16 ounces) frozen mixed vegetables
     (carrots, potatoes and peas)
 1 jar (4½ ounces) sliced mushrooms, drained
 1 package (6.2 ounces) long grain and wild rice
 2 teaspoons lemon juice
 ⅛ teaspoon ground nutmeg
   Salt and pepper to taste
```

Heat oil in large skillet over high heat. Add pork, onion, celery, basil, rosemary and oregano. Cook until pork is browned. Place pork mixture in slow cooker. Stir flour into chicken broth; pour into slow cooker.

Stir in frozen vegetables and mushrooms. Cover and cook on LOW 4 hours or until pork is barely pink in center. Prepare rice according to package directions, discarding spice packet, if desired.

Stir lemon juice, nutmeg and salt and pepper to taste into slow cooker. Cover and cook 15 minutes. Serve stew over rice.
Makes 4 (1-cup) servings

Bad

Beer and Cheese Soup

 2 to 3 slices pumpernickel or rye bread
¼ cup finely chopped onion
 2 cloves garlic, minced
¾ teaspoon dried thyme leaves
 1 can (about 14 ounces) chicken broth
 1 cup beer
 6 ounces American cheese, shredded or diced
 4 to 6 ounces sharp Cheddar cheese, shredded
½ teaspoon paprika
 1 cup milk

Preheat oven to 425°F. Slice bread into ½-inch cubes; place on baking sheet. Bake 10 to 12 minutes, stirring once, or until crisp; set aside.

Combine onion, garlic, thyme, chicken broth and beer in slow cooker. Cover and cook on LOW 4 hours. Turn to HIGH. Stir cheeses, paprika and milk into slow cooker. Cook 45 to 60 minutes or until soup is hot and cheeses are melted. Stir soup well to blend cheeses. Ladle soup into bowls; top with pumpernickel croutons.   *Makes 4 (1-cup) servings*

Beer and Cheese Soup

Italian Sausage and Vegetable Stew

1 pound hot or mild Italian sausage, cut into 1-inch pieces
1 package (16 ounces) frozen mixed vegetables (onions and
    green, red and yellow bell peppers)
1 can (14½ ounces) diced Italian-style tomatoes, undrained
2 medium zucchini, sliced
1 jar (4½ ounces) sliced mushrooms, drained
4 cloves garlic, minced
2 tablespoons Italian-style tomato paste

Heat large skillet over high heat until hot. Add sausage; cook about
5 minutes or until browned. Pour off any drippings.

Combine sausage, frozen vegetables, tomatoes, zucchini, mushrooms
and garlic in slow cooker. Cover and cook on LOW 4 to 4½ hours or
until zucchini is tender. Stir in tomato paste. Cover and cook 30
minutes or until juices have thickened.   *Makes 6 (1-cup) servings*

Serving Suggestion: Italian Sausage and Vegetable Stew is excellent
served with garlic bread.

*Italian Sausage and
Vegetable Stew*

Jambalaya

2 cups diced boiled ham
2 medium onions, coarsely chopped
2 stalks celery, sliced
½ green bell pepper, seeded and diced
1 can (28 ounces) whole tomatoes
¼ cup tomato paste
3 cloves garlic, minced
1 tablespoon minced parsley
½ teaspoon dried thyme leaves
2 whole cloves
2 tablespoons vegetable oil
1 cup uncooked long-grain converted rice
1 pound fresh or frozen shrimp, shelled and deveined

SLOW COOKER DIRECTIONS
Thoroughly mix all ingredients *except* shrimp in CROCK-POT® Slow Cooker. Cover and cook on Low 8 to 10 hours.

One hour before serving, turn CROCK-POT® Slow Cooker to High. Stir in uncooked shrimp. Cover and cook until shrimp are pink and tender.
Makes 4 to 6 servings

Chicken Stew with Dumplings

2 cups sliced carrots
1 cup chopped onion
1 large green bell pepper, sliced
½ cup sliced celery
2 cans (about 14 ounces *each*) chicken broth
⅔ cup all-purpose flour
1 pound boneless skinless chicken breasts, cut into 1-inch pieces
1 large potato, unpeeled and cut into 1-inch pieces
6 ounces mushrooms, halved
¾ cup frozen peas
1 teaspoon dried basil
¾ teaspoon dried rosemary
¼ teaspoon dried tarragon
¾ to 1 teaspoon salt
¼ teaspoon black pepper
¼ cup heavy cream

HERB DUMPLINGS
1 cup biscuit mix
¼ teaspoon dried basil
¼ teaspoon dried rosemary
⅛ teaspoon dried tarragon
⅓ cup reduced-fat (2%) milk

For stew, combine carrots, onion, bell pepper and celery in slow cooker. Stir in chicken broth, reserving 1 cup broth. Cover and cook on LOW 2 hours.

Stir flour into remaining 1 cup broth until smooth. Stir into slow cooker. Add chicken, potato, mushrooms, peas, basil, rosemary and tarragon to slow cooker. Cover and cook 4 hours or until vegetables are tender and chicken is no longer pink. Stir in salt, black pepper and heavy cream.

For dumplings, combine biscuit mix and herbs in small bowl. Stir in milk to form soft dough. Spoon dumpling mixture on top of stew in 4 large spoonfuls. Cook, uncovered, 30 minutes. Cover and cook 30 to 45 minutes or until dumplings are firm and toothpick inserted in center comes out clean. Serve in shallow bowls. *Makes 4 servings*

Chicken Stew with Dumpling

Chinese Chicken Stew

1 pound boneless skinless chicken thighs, cut into 1-inch pieces
1 teaspoon Chinese five-spice powder
½ to ¾ teaspoon red pepper flakes
1 tablespoon peanut or vegetable oil
1 large onion, coarsely chopped
1 package (8 ounces) fresh mushrooms, sliced
2 cloves garlic, minced
1 can (about 14 ounces) chicken broth, divided
1 tablespoon cornstarch
1 large red bell pepper, cut into ¾-inch pieces
2 tablespoons soy sauce
1 tablespoon sesame oil
2 large green onions, cut into ½-inch pieces
3 cups hot cooked white rice (optional)
¼ cup coarsely chopped cilantro (optional)

Toss chicken with five-spice powder in small bowl. Season with red pepper flakes. Heat peanut oil in large skillet. Add onion and chicken; cook and stir about 5 minutes or until chicken is browned. Add mushrooms and garlic; cook and stir until chicken is no longer pink.

Combine ¼ cup broth and cornstarch in small bowl; set aside. Place cooked chicken mixture, remaining broth, bell pepper and soy sauce in slow cooker. Cover and cook on LOW 3½ hours or until peppers are tender.

Stir in cornstarch mixture, sesame oil and green onions; cook 30 to 45 minutes or until juices have thickened. Ladle into soup bowls; scoop ½ cup rice into each bowl, if desired. Sprinkle with cilantro, if desired.

Makes 6 servings (about 5 cups)

Chinese Chicken Stew

Classic French Onion Soup

¼ cup butter
3 large yellow onions, sliced
1 cup dry white wine
3 cans (about 14 ounces *each*) beef or chicken broth
½ teaspoon dried thyme
½ teaspoon salt
1 teaspoon Worcestershire sauce
1 loaf French bread, sliced and toasted
4 ounces shredded Swiss cheese
Fresh thyme for garnish

Melt butter in large skillet over high heat. Add onions; cook and stir 15 minutes or until onions are soft and lightly browned. Stir in wine.

Combine onion mixture, beef broth, thyme, salt and Worcestershire in slow cooker. Cover and cook on LOW 4 to 4½ hours. Ladle soup into 4 individual bowls; top with bread slice and cheese. Garnish with fresh thyme, if desired.   *Makes 4 servings*

Classic French Onion Soup

Smoked Sausage Gumbo

1 cup chicken broth
1 can (14½ ounces) diced tomatoes, undrained
¼ cup all-purpose flour
2 tablespoons olive oil
¾ pound Polish sausage, cut into ½-inch pieces
1 medium onion, diced
1 green bell pepper, diced
2 ribs celery, chopped
1 carrot, peeled and chopped
2 teaspoons dried oregano
2 teaspoons dried thyme
⅛ teaspoon ground red pepper
1 cup uncooked long-grain white rice

Combine broth and tomatoes in slow cooker. Sprinkle flour evenly over bottom of small skillet. Cook over high heat without stirring 3 to 4 minutes or until flour begins to brown. Reduce heat to medium; stir flour about 4 minutes. Stir in oil until smooth. Carefully whisk flour mixture into slow cooker.

Add sausage, onion, bell pepper, celery, carrot, oregano, thyme and ground red pepper to slow cooker. Stir well. Cover and cook on LOW 4½ to 5 hours or until juices are thickened.

About 30 minutes before gumbo is ready to serve, prepare rice. Cook rice in 2 cups boiling water in medium saucepan. Serve gumbo over rice.   *Makes 4 servings*

Note: For a special touch, sprinkle chopped parsley over each serving.

Smoked Sausage Gumbo

Pipin' Hot Poultry

Chicken Fajita with Cowpoke Barbecue Sauce (page 42)

Chicken Fajitas with Cowpoke Barbecue Sauce

COWPOKE BARBECUE SAUCE
- ¾ cup chopped green onions
- 3 cloves garlic, minced
- 1 can (14½ ounces) crushed tomatoes
- ½ cup ketchup
- ¼ cup water
- ¼ cup orange juice
- 2 tablespoons cider vinegar
- 2 teaspoons chili sauce
- Dash Worcestershire sauce

CHICKEN FAJITAS
- 10 ounces boneless skinless chicken breasts, cut lengthwise into 1×½-inch pieces
- 2 green or red bell peppers, thinly sliced
- 1 cup sliced onion
- 2 cups tomato wedges
- 4 (6-inch) warm flour tortillas

Combine all Cowpoke Barbecue Sauce ingredients in slow cooker. Cover and cook on HIGH 1½ hours.

Spray large nonstick skillet with nonstick cooking spray. Add chicken and cook over medium heat until browned. Reduce slow cooker heat to LOW. Add cooked chicken, bell peppers and onion to slow cooker. Stir until well coated. Cover and cook 3 to 4 hours or until chicken is no longer pink and vegetables are tender.

Add tomatoes; cover and cook 30 to 45 minutes or until heated through. Serve with warm tortillas. *Makes 4 servings*

Lemony Roasted Chicken

- 1 fryer or roasting chicken (3 to 4 pounds)
- ½ cup chopped onion
- 2 tablespoons butter
- Juice of one lemon
- 1 tablespoon fresh parsley
- 2 teaspoons grated lemon peel
- ¼ teaspoon salt
- ¼ teaspoon dried thyme leaves

Rinse chicken and pat dry with paper towels. Remove and discard any excess fat. Place onion in chicken cavity and rub skin with butter. Place chicken in slow cooker. Squeeze juice of lemon over chicken. Sprinkle with parsley, grated lemon peel, salt and thyme. Cover and cook on LOW 6 to 8 hours. *Makes 6 servings*

Harvest Drums

    1 package (about 1¼ pounds) PERDUE® Fresh Skinless Chicken
        Drumsticks
    ½ teaspoon dried Italian herb seasoning
        Salt and black pepper
    3 bacon slices, diced
    2 cans (14½ ounces each) pasta-ready tomatoes with cheeses
    1 small onion, chopped
    1 garlic clove, minced
    ¼ cup red wine
    1 small zucchini, scrubbed and julienned
    1 package (12 ounces) angel hair pasta, cooked and drained

Sprinkle chicken with Italian seasoning and salt and pepper to taste. In large, nonstick skillet over medium-low heat, cook bacon about 5 minutes, until crisp. Remove from skillet; drain and crumble. Increase heat to medium-high. Add chicken to bacon drippings (or replace drippings with 1½ tablespoons olive oil); cook 4 to 5 minutes on all sides or until brown, turning often.

In large slow cooker, combine tomatoes, bacon, onion, garlic and wine. Add chicken; cook on high 1½ to 1¾ hours, or until fork-tender. Add zucchini during last 5 minutes of cooking. Serve chicken and vegetables over angel hair pasta. *Makes 3 to 4 servings*

Chicken Curry

1 small onion, sliced
2 boneless skinless chicken breast halves, cut into ¾-inch pieces
1 clove garlic, minced
1 teaspoon curry powder
¼ teaspoon ground ginger
3 tablespoons raisins
1 cup coarsely chopped apple, divided
1½ teaspoons chicken bouillon granules
1½ teaspoons all-purpose flour
⅓ cup water
¼ cup sour cream
½ teaspoon cornstarch
½ cup uncooked white rice

Combine onion, chicken, garlic, curry powder, ginger, raisins and ¾ cup chopped apple in slow cooker. Combine chicken bouillon granules, flour and water in small bowl; stir until dissolved. Add to slow cooker. Cover and cook on LOW 3½ to 4 hours or until onions are tender and chicken is no longer pink.

Combine sour cream and cornstarch in large bowl. Turn off slow cooker; remove insert to heatproof surface. Drain all cooking liquid from chicken mixture and stir into sour cream mixture. Add back to insert; stir well. Place insert back in slow cooker. Cover and let stand 5 to 10 minutes or until sauce is heated through.

Meanwhile, cook rice according to package directions. Serve chicken curry over rice; garnish with remaining ¼ cup apple.

Makes 2 servings

Note: For a special touch, sprinkle chicken with with green onion slivers just before serving.

Chicken Curry

Fusilli Pizzaiola with Turkey Meatballs

   2 cans (14½ ounces *each*) no-salt-added tomatoes, undrained
   1 can (8 ounces) no-salt-added tomato sauce
   ¼ cup chopped onion
   ¼ cup grated carrot
   2 tablespoons no-salt-added tomato paste
   2 tablespoons chopped fresh basil
   1 clove garlic, minced
   ½ teaspoon dried thyme leaves
   ¼ teaspoon sugar
   ¼ teaspoon black pepper, divided
   1 bay leaf
   1 pound ground turkey breast
   1 egg, lightly beaten
   1 tablespoon fat-free (skim) milk
   ¼ cup Italian-seasoned dry bread crumbs
   2 tablespoons chopped fresh parsley
   8 ounces uncooked fusilli or other spiral-shaped pasta

Combine tomatoes, tomato sauce, onion, carrot, tomato paste, basil, garlic, thyme, sugar, ⅛ teaspoon black pepper and bay leaf in slow cooker. Break up tomatoes gently with wooden spoon. Cover and cook on LOW 4½ to 5 hours.

About 45 minutes before end of cooking, prepare meatballs. Preheat oven to 350°F. Combine turkey, egg and milk; blend in bread crumbs, parsley and remaining ⅛ teaspoon black pepper. With wet hands, shape mixture into small balls. Spray baking sheet with nonstick cooking spray. Arrange meatballs on baking sheet. Bake 25 minutes or until no longer pink in center.

Add meatballs to slow cooker. Cover and cook 45 minutes to 1 hour or until meatballs are heated through. Discard bay leaf. Prepare pasta according to package directions. Drain. Place in serving bowl; top with meatballs and sauce. *Makes 4 servings*

Fusilli Pizzaiola with Turkey Meatballs

90's-Style Slow Cooker Coq Au Vin

2 packages BUTTERBALL® Boneless Skinless Chicken Breast Fillets
1 pound fresh mushrooms, sliced thick
1 jar (15 ounces) pearl onions, drained
½ cup dry white wine
1 teaspoon thyme leaves
1 bay leaf
1 cup chicken broth
⅓ cup flour
½ cup chopped fresh parsley
   Wild rice pilaf (optional)

SLOW COOKER DIRECTIONS
Place chicken, mushrooms, onions, wine, thyme and bay leaf into slow cooker. Combine chicken broth and flour; pour into slow cooker. Cover and cook 5 hours on low setting. Add parsley. Serve over wild rice pilaf, if desired. *Makes 8 servings*

Preparation Time: 30 minutes plus cooking time

He-Man Stew

1 package (about 3½ pounds) PERDUE® Fresh Skinless Pick of the Chicken
   Salt and ground pepper
2 tablespoons olive oil
1 can (12 ounces) lite beer
1 can (28 ounces) whole plum tomatoes, drained and chopped
1 onion, sliced into rings
¼ cup spicy brown mustard
4 cups cooked elbow macaroni

Season chicken with salt and pepper to taste. In large nonstick skillet over medium-high heat, heat oil. Add chicken; cook 5 to 6 minutes on each side for larger pieces, 3 to 4 minutes on each side for smaller pieces, or until brown, turning often. In large slow cooker, combine beer, tomatoes, onion and mustard. Add chicken. Cook on high 1½ to 2 hours, or until chicken is fork-tender. Serve over macaroni. *Makes 3 to 4 servings*

Turkey Tacos

     1 pound ground turkey
     1 medium onion, chopped
     1 can (6 ounces) tomato paste
     ½ cup chunky salsa
     1 tablespoon chopped cilantro
     ½ teaspoon salt
     8 taco shells
     1 tablespoon butter
     1 tablespoon all-purpose flour
     ¼ teaspoon salt
     ⅓ cup milk
     ½ cup sour cream
        Ground red pepper

Brown turkey and onion in large skillet over medium heat. Combine turkey mixture, tomato paste, salsa, cilantro and salt in slow cooker. Cover and cook on LOW 4 to 5 hours. Spoon ¼ cup turkey mixture into each taco shell; keep warm.

Melt butter in small saucepan over low heat. Stir in flour and salt. Carefully stir in milk. Cook over low heat until thickened. Remove from heat. Combine sour cream and sprinkle of ground red pepper in small bowl. Stir into hot milk mixture. Return to heat; cook over low heat 1 minute, stirring constantly. Spoon over taco filling.   *Makes 8 tacos*

Meatball Grinders

¼ cup chopped onion
1 can (15 ounces) diced tomatoes, drained and juice reserved
1 can (8 ounces) reduced-sodium tomato sauce
2 tablespoons tomato paste
1 teaspoon dried Italian seasoning
1 pound ground chicken
½ cup fresh whole-wheat or white bread crumbs (1 slice bread)
1 egg white, lightly beaten
3 tablespoons finely chopped fresh parsley
2 cloves garlic, minced
¼ teaspoon salt
⅛ teaspoon black pepper
4 small hard rolls, split
2 tablespoons grated Parmesan cheese

Combine onion, diced tomatoes, ½ cup reserved juice, tomato sauce, tomato paste and Italian seasoning in slow cooker. Cover and cook on LOW 3 to 4 hours or until onions are soft.

During the last 30 minutes of cooking time, prepare meatballs. Combine chicken, bread crumbs, egg white, parsley, garlic, salt and pepper in medium bowl. With wet hands form mixture into 12 to 16 meatballs. Spray medium nonstick skillet with cooking spray; heat over medium heat until hot. Add meatballs; cook about 8 to 10 minutes or until well browned on all sides. Remove meatballs to slow cooker; cook 1 to 2 hours or until meatballs are no longer pink in centers and are heated through.

Place 3 to 4 meatballs in each roll. Divide sauce evenly; spoon over meatballs. Sprinkle with cheese.   *Makes 4 servings*

Meatball Grinder

Greek-Style Chicken Stew

    2 cups cubed peeled eggplant
    2 cups sliced mushrooms
    ¾ cup coarsely chopped onion
    2 cloves garlic, minced
    1 teaspoon dried oregano leaves
    ½ teaspoon dried basil leaves
    ½ teaspoon dried thyme leaves
    1¼ cups low-sodium chicken broth
    1½ teaspoons all-purpose flour
    6 skinless chicken breasts (about 2 pounds)
        Additional all-purpose flour
    3 tablespoons dry sherry or low-sodium chicken broth
    ¼ teaspoon salt
    ¼ teaspoon black pepper
    1 can (14 ounces) artichoke hearts, drained
    12 ounces uncooked wide egg noodles

Combine eggplant, mushrooms, onion, garlic, oregano, basil, thyme, broth and flour in slow cooker. Cover and cook on HIGH 1 hour.

Coat chicken very lightly with flour. Generously spray large nonstick skillet with cooking spray; heat over medium heat until hot. Cook chicken 10 to 15 minutes or until browned on all sides.

Remove vegetables to bowl with slotted spoon. Layer chicken in slow cooker; return vegetables to slow cooker. Add sherry, salt and pepper. Reduce heat to LOW and cover and cook 6 to 6½ hours or until chicken is no longer pink in center and vegetables are tender.

Stir in artichokes; cover and cook 45 minutes to 1 hour or until heated through. Cook noodles according to package directions. Serve chicken stew over noodles. *Makes 6 servings*

Greek-Style Chicken Stew

Beef & Pork

Broccoli and Beef Pasta (page 56)

Broccoli and Beef Pasta

2 cups broccoli florets *or* 1 package (10 ounces) frozen broccoli, thawed
1 medium onion, thinly sliced
½ teaspoon dried basil leaves
½ teaspoon dried oregano leaves
½ teaspoon dried thyme leaves
1 can (14½ ounces) Italian-style diced tomatoes, undrained
¾ cup beef broth
1 pound lean ground beef
2 cloves garlic, minced
2 tablespoons tomato paste
2 cups cooked rotini pasta
3 ounces shredded Cheddar cheese or grated Parmesan cheese

Layer broccoli, onion, basil, oregano, thyme, tomatoes and beef broth in slow cooker. Cover and cook on LOW 2½ hours.

Combine beef and garlic in large nonstick skillet; cook over high heat 6 to 8 minutes or until meat is no longer pink, breaking meat apart with wooden spoon. Pour off drippings. Add beef mixture to slow cooker. Cover and cook 2 hours.

Stir in tomato paste. Add pasta and cheese. Cover and cook 30 minutes or until cheese melts and mixture is heated through.

Makes 4 servings

Glazed Corned Beef

1½ **cups water**
1 **medium onion, sliced**
3 **strips fresh orange peel**
2 **whole cloves**
3 **to 4 pounds corned beef (round or rump cut)**
   Additional whole cloves (optional)
   Glaze (recipe follows)

Combine water, onion, orange peel and cloves in slow cooker. Add corned beef, fat side up, to slow cooker. Cover and cook on LOW 7 to 9 hours or until fork-tender.

Remove corned beef from slow cooker. Score top of corned beef; insert additional cloves to decorate, if desired.

About 30 minutes before serving, place corned beef in ovenproof pan. Preheat oven to 375°F. Prepare Glaze; spoon over corned beef. Bake 20 to 30 minutes, basting occasionally with Glaze.

Makes 8 to 10 servings

Glaze

3 **tablespoons honey**
2 **tablespoons frozen orange juice concentrate, thawed**
2 **teaspoons prepared mustard**

Combine honey, orange juice concentrate and mustard in large bowl.

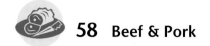
Barbecued Beef

    3 pounds boneless chuck roast
1½ cups ketchup
 ¼ cup packed brown sugar
 ¼ cup red wine vinegar
  2 tablespoons Dijon-style mustard
  2 tablespoons Worcestershire sauce
  1 teaspoon liquid smoke flavoring
 ½ teaspoon salt
 ¼ teaspoon black pepper
 ¼ teaspoon garlic powder
    Sandwich buns

SLOW COOKER DIRECTIONS

Place chuck roast in CROCK-POT® Slow Cooker. Combine remaining ingredients in large bowl. Pour barbecue sauce mixture over chuck roast. Cover and cook on Low 8 to 10 hours or 4 to 5 hours on High. Remove chuck roast from CROCK-POT® Slow Cooker; shred meat with fork. Place shredded meat back in CROCK-POT® Slow Cooker. Stir meat to evenly coat with sauce. Spoon meat onto sandwich buns and top with additional barbecue sauce, if desired.   *Makes 12 servings*

Vegetable-Stuffed Pork Chops

    4 double pork loin chops, well trimmed
      Salt and black pepper
    1 can (15¼ ounces) corn, drained
    1 small onion, chopped
    1 green bell pepper, seeded and chopped
    1 cup Italian-style seasoned dry bread crumbs
   ½ cup uncooked, long-grain converted rice
    1 can (8 ounces) tomato sauce
      Fresh salad (optional)

Cut pocket in each pork chop, cutting from edge nearest bone. Lightly season pockets with salt and pepper to taste. Combine corn, onion, bell pepper, bread crumbs and rice in large bowl. Stuff pork chops with vegetable-rice mixture. Secure along fat side with wooden toothpicks.

Pour any remaining vegetable-rice mixture into slow cooker. Add stuffed pork chops to slow cooker. Moisten top of each pork chop with tomato sauce. Pour any remaining tomato sauce over top. Cover and cook on LOW 8 to 10 hours or until done.

Remove pork chops to serving platter. Serve with vegetable-rice mixture and fresh salad, if desired. *Makes 4 servings*

Beefy Tostada Pies

2 teaspoons olive oil
1½ cups chopped onions
2 pounds ground beef
1 teaspoon chili powder
1 teaspoon ground cumin
1 teaspoon salt
2 cloves garlic, minced
1 can (15 ounces) tomato sauce
1 cup sliced black olives
8 flour tortillas
4 cups shredded Cheddar cheese
Sour cream, salsa and chopped green onion (optional)

Heat oil in large skillet over medium heat. Add onions and cook until tender. Add ground beef, chili powder, cumin, salt and garlic; cook until browned. Stir in tomato sauce; heat through. Stir in black olives.

Make foil handles using three 18×2-inch strips of heavy foil. Crisscross foil to form spoke design. Place in slow cooker. Lay one tortilla on foil strips. Spread with meat sauce and layer of cheese. Top with another tortilla, meat sauce and cheese. Repeat layers ending with cheese. Cover and cook on HIGH 1½ hours. To serve, lift out of slow cooker using foil handles and transfer to serving platter. Discard foil. Cut into wedges. Serve with sour cream, salsa and chopped green onion, if desired.   *Makes 4 to 5 servings*

Give Me a Side of. . .

Arroz con Queso (page 64)

Arroz con Queso

1 can (16 ounces) whole tomatoes, mashed
1 can (16 ounces) Mexican-style beans
1½ cups uncooked long-grain converted rice
1 large onion, finely chopped
1 cup cottage cheese
1 can (4 ounces) green chili peppers, drained, seeded and chopped
2 tablespoons vegetable oil
3 cloves garlic, minced
2 cups grated Monterey Jack or processed cheese, divided

SLOW COOKER DIRECTIONS

Lightly grease CROCK-POT® Slow Cooker. Mix all ingredients *except* 1 cup grated cheese in large bowl. Pour mixture into CROCK-POT® Slow Cooker. Cover and cook on Low 6 to 9 hours.

Just before serving, sprinkle with reserved grated cheese.

Makes 6 to 8 servings

Mrs. Grady's Beans

½ pound lean ground beef
1 small onion, chopped
8 bacon strips, chopped
1 can (about 15 ounces) pinto beans, undrained
1 can (about 15 ounces) butter beans, rinsed and drained, reserving ¼ cup liquid
1 can (about 15 ounces) kidney beans, rinsed and drained
¼ cup ketchup
2 tablespoons molasses
½ teaspoon dry mustard
½ cup granulated sugar
¼ cup packed brown sugar

Brown ground beef, onion and bacon in medium saucepan over high heat. Stir in beans and liquid; set aside.

Combine ketchup, molasses and mustard in medium bowl. Mix in sugars. Stir ketchup mixture into beef mixture; mix well. Transfer to slow cooker. Cover and cook on LOW 2 to 3 hours or until heated through. *Makes 6 to 8 servings*

Sunshine Squash

 1 butternut squash (about 2 pounds) peeled, seeded and diced
 1 can (14½ ounces) tomatoes, undrained
 1 can (about 15 ounces) corn, drained
 1 medium onion, coarsely chopped
 1 clove garlic, minced
 1 green bell pepper, seeded and cut into 1-inch pieces
 1 canned green chili, coarsely chopped
 ½ cup chicken broth
 ½ teaspoon salt
 ¼ teaspoon black pepper
 1 tablespoon plus 1½ teaspoons tomato paste

Combine all ingredients *except* tomato paste in slow cooker. Cover and cook on LOW 6 hours or until squash is tender.

Remove about ¼ cup cooking liquid and blend with tomato paste. Stir into slow cooker. Cook 30 minutes or until mixture is slightly thickened and heated through. *Makes 6 to 8 servings*

Louise's Broccoli Casserole

2 packages (10 ounces each) frozen broccoli spears, thawed and
    cut up
1 can (10¾ ounces) condensed cream of celery soup
1¼ cups grated sharp Cheddar cheese, divided
¼ cup minced green onions
1 cup crushed saltine crackers or potato chips

SLOW COOKER DIRECTIONS
Grease CROCK-POT® Slow Cooker. In large bowl, combine broccoli,
celery soup, 1 cup cheese and onions. Pour into CROCK-POT® Slow
Cooker. Sprinkle top with crushed crackers, then with remaining cheese.
Cover and cook on Low 5 to 6 hours or on High 2½ to 3 hours.

Makes 4 to 6 servings

Note: If desired, casserole may be spooned into a baking dish and
garnished with additional grated cheese and broken potato chips; bake
5 to 10 minutes in 400°F oven.

Louise's Broccoli Casserole

Bean and Cornbread Casserole

1 medium onion, chopped
1 medium green bell pepper, chopped
2 cloves garlic, minced *or* ¼ teaspoon garlic powder
1 can (16 ounces) red kidney beans, undrained
1 can (16 ounces) pinto beans, undrained
1 can (16 ounces) no-salt-added diced tomatoes, undrained
1 can (8 ounces) no-salt-added tomato sauce
1 teaspoon chili powder
½ teaspoon black pepper
½ teaspoon prepared mustard
⅛ teaspoon hot sauce
1 cup yellow cornmeal
1 cup all-purpose flour
2½ teaspoons baking powder
1 tablespoon sugar
½ teaspoon salt
1¼ cups milk
½ cup egg substitute
3 tablespoons vegetable oil
1 can (8½ ounces) no-salt-added cream-style corn

SLOW COOKER DIRECTIONS

Lightly grease CROCK-POT® Slow Cooker. In skillet over medium heat, cook onion, bell pepper and garlic until tender. Transfer to CROCK-POT® Slow Cooker. Stir in kidney beans and pinto beans. Add diced tomatoes and juice, tomato sauce, seasonings, mustard and hot sauce. Cover and cook on High for 1 hour.

In large bowl, combine cornmeal, flour, baking powder, sugar and salt. Stir in milk, egg substitute, vegetable oil and corn. Spoon evenly over bean mixture. There may be leftover cornbread depending on size of CROCK-POT® Slow Cooker being used (if there's remaining cornbread, spoon into greased muffin tins and bake at 375°F 30 minutes or until golden brown). Cover and cook on High 1½ to 2 more hours. Serve.

Makes 6 to 8 servings

New England Baked Beans

4 slices uncooked bacon, chopped
3 cans (15 ounces *each*) Great Northern beans, rinsed and
    drained
¾ cup water
1 small onion, chopped
2 cloves garlic, minced
3 tablespoons firmly packed brown sugar
3 tablespoons maple syrup
3 tablespoons unsulphured molasses
½ teaspoon salt
½ teaspoon dry mustard
⅛ teaspoon black pepper
½ bay leaf
⅓ cup canned diced tomatoes, well drained

Cook bacon in large skillet until almost cooked but not crispy. Drain on paper towels.

Combine bacon and all remaining ingredients in slow cooker. Cover and cook on LOW 6 to 8 hours or until onions are tender and mixture is thickened. Remove bay leaf before serving.   *Makes 4 to 6 servings*

New England Baked Beans

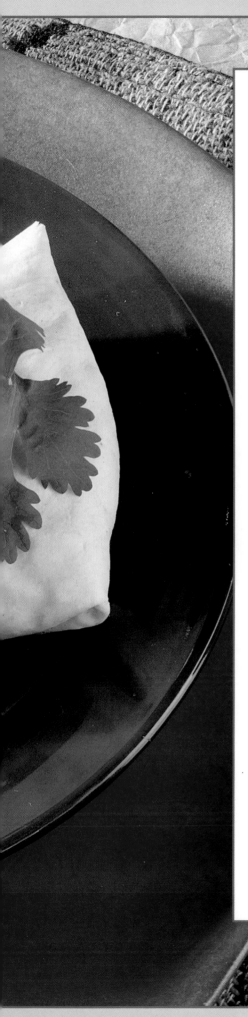

Totally Vegetarian

Bean and Vegetable Burrito (page 74)

Bean and Vegetable Burritos

2 tablespoons chili powder
2 teaspoons dried oregano leaves
1½ teaspoons ground cumin
1 large sweet potato, peeled and diced
1 can black beans or pinto beans, rinsed and drained
4 cloves garlic, minced
1 medium onion, halved and thinly sliced
1 jalapeño pepper, seeded and minced
1 green bell pepper, chopped
1 cup frozen corn, thawed and drained
3 tablespoons lime juice
1 tablespoon chopped cilantro
¾ cup (3 ounces) shredded Monterey Jack cheese
4 (10-inch) flour tortillas
Sour cream (optional)

* Jalapeño peppers can sting and irritate the skin; wear rubber gloves when handling peppers and do not touch eyes. Wash hands after handling.

Combine chili powder, oregano and cumin in small bowl. Set aside.

Layer sweet potato, beans, half of chili powder mix, garlic, onion, jalapeño pepper, bell pepper, remaining half of chili powder mix and corn in slow cooker. Cover and cook on LOW 5 hours or until sweet potato is tender. Stir in lime juice and cilantro.

Preheat oven to 350°F. Spoon 2 tablespoons cheese in center of each tortilla. Top with 1 cup filling. Fold all 4 sides to enclose filling. Place burritos seam side down on baking sheet. Cover with foil and bake 20 to 30 minutes or until heated through. Serve with sour cream, if desired. *Makes 4 servings*

Meatless Sloppy Joes

2 cups thinly sliced onions
2 cups chopped green bell peppers
1 can (about 15 ounces) kidney beans, drained and mashed
1 can (8 ounces) tomato sauce
2 cloves garlic, finely chopped
2 tablespoons ketchup
1 tablespoon mustard
1 teaspoon chili powder
   Cider vinegar (optional)
4 sandwich rolls, halved

Combine all ingredients *except* rolls in slow cooker. Cover and cook on LOW 5 to 5½ hours or until vegetables are tender. Serve on rolls.

Makes 4 servings

Pesto Rice and Beans

1 can (15 ounces) Great Northern beans, rinsed and drained
1 can (14 ounces) vegetable broth
¾ cup uncooked long-grain white rice
1½ cups frozen cut green beans, thawed and drained
½ cup prepared pesto sauce
   Additional grated Parmesan cheese (optional)

Combine Great Northern beans, vegetable broth and rice in slow cooker. Cover and cook on LOW 2 hours.

Stir in green beans; cover and cook 1 hour or until rice and beans are tender. Turn off slow cooker and remove insert to heatproof surface. Stir in pesto sauce and additional Parmesan cheese, if desired. Let stand, covered, 5 minutes or until cheese has melted. Serve immediately.

Makes 8 servings

Savory Bean Stew

1 cup frozen vegetable seasoning blend (onions, celery, red and green bell peppers)
1 can (15½ ounces) chick-peas, rinsed and drained
1 can (15 ounces) pinto beans, rinsed and drained
1 can (15 ounces) black beans, rinsed and drained
1 can (14½ ounces) diced tomatoes with roasted garlic, undrained
¾ teaspoon dried thyme leaves
¾ teaspoon dried sage leaves
½ to ¾ teaspoon dried oregano leaves
1 tablespoon all-purpose flour
¾ cup vegetable broth, divided

POLENTA
¾ cup yellow cornmeal
¾ teaspoon salt

Combine frozen vegetable blend, chick-peas, beans, tomatoes and herbs in slow cooker. Stir flour into ½ cup vegetable broth; pour into bean mixture and stir well. Cover and cook 4 hours or until vegetables are tender and juice is thickened.

Meanwhile, prepare polenta. Bring 3 cups water to a boil in large saucepan. Reduce heat; gradually stir in cornmeal and salt. Cook 5 to 8 minutes or until cornmeal thickens. Keep warm.

Stir remaining ¼ cup broth into slow cooker. Spread polenta on plate and top with stew.   *Makes 6 (1-cup) servings*

Savory Bean Stew

Savory Bean Stew with Cheddar-Cornmeal Dumplings

1 can (28 ounces) tomatoes, undrained and chopped
2 cups chopped red bell peppers
1 can (15 ounces) black beans, rinsed and drained
1 can (15 ounces) pinto beans, rinsed and drained
2 small zucchini, coarsely chopped
2 large onions, chopped
1 poblano chili, seeded and chopped
½ cup sliced celery
3 cloves garlic, minced
3 tablespoons chili powder
2 teaspoons ground cumin
1 teaspoon dried oregano leaves
½ teaspoon salt, divided
½ cup all-purpose flour
½ cup cornmeal
1 teaspoon baking powder
½ teaspoon sugar
2 tablespoons cold butter or margarine
¼ cup shredded Cheddar cheese
1 tablespoon minced fresh cilantro
½ cup milk

Combine tomatoes, red bell peppers, beans, zucchini, onions, poblano chili, celery, garlic, chili powder, cumin, oregano, and ¼ teaspoon salt in slow cooker. Cover and cook on HIGH 4 to 4½ hours or until vegetables are tender.

During the last hour of cooking, prepare dumplings. Combine flour, cornmeal, baking powder, sugar and remaining ¼ teaspoon salt in medium bowl. Cut in butter with pastry blender or two knives until mixture resembles coarse crumbs.

Stir in cheese and cilantro. Pour milk into flour mixture; blend with wooden spoon just until dry ingredients are moistened. Drop dumpling dough into 6 mounds on top of stew. Cover and cook 40 minutes to 1 hour or until toothpick inserted into dumplings comes out clean.

Makes 6 servings

*Savory Bean Stew with
Cheddar-Cornmeal Dumplings*

Sweet Potato Casserole

 2 cans (18 ounces *each*) sweet potatoes, drained and mashed
⅓ cup margarine or butter, melted
 2 tablespoons granulated sugar
 2 tablespoons plus ⅓ cup brown sugar, divided
 1 tablespoon orange juice
 2 eggs, beaten
½ cup milk
⅓ cup chopped pecans
 2 tablespoons all-purpose flour
 2 tablespoons margarine or butter, melted

SLOW COOKER DIRECTIONS

Lightly grease CROCK-POT® Slow Cooker. Mix sweet potatoes, ⅓ cup margarine, granulated sugar and 2 tablespoons brown sugar in large bowl. Beat in orange juice, eggs and milk. Transfer to CROCK-POT® Slow Cooker.

Combine pecans, ⅓ cup brown sugar, flour and 2 tablespoons margarine. Spread over sweet potatoes. Cover and cook on High 3 to 4 hours. Serve. *Makes 6 to 8 servings*

Slow Cooker & More

Soups, Stews, Main Dishes & More

Plus **Winter Warm-ups & Hearty Meals**

Contents

In the Soup

Fiesta Black Bean Soup

Slow Cooker Recipe

    6 cups chicken broth
    1 can (16 ounces) black beans, drained
  ¾ pound potatoes, peeled and diced
  ½ pound ham, diced
  ½ onion, diced
    1 can (4 ounces) chopped jalapeño peppers
    2 cloves garlic, minced
    2 teaspoons dried oregano leaves
1½ teaspoons dried thyme leaves
    1 teaspoon ground cumin
      Sour cream, chopped bell peppers and chopped tomatoes
        for garnish

Combine all ingredients, except garnish, in slow cooker. Cover and cook on Low 8 to 10 hours or on High 4 to 5 hours. Garnish, if desired.   *Makes 6 to 8 servings*

Fiesta Black Bean Soup

82

Potato and Leek Soup

Slow Cooker Recipe

4 cups chicken broth
3 potatoes, peeled and diced
1½ cups chopped cabbage
1 leek, diced
1 onion, chopped
2 carrots, diced
¼ cup chopped parsley
2 teaspoons salt
2 teaspoons black pepper
½ teaspoon caraway seeds
1 bay leaf
½ cup sour cream
1 pound bacon, cooked and crumbled

Combine chicken broth, potatoes, cabbage, leek, onion, carrots and parsley in large bowl; pour mixture into slow cooker. Stir in salt, pepper, caraway seeds and bay leaf. Cover and cook on Low 8 to 10 hours or on High 4 to 5 hours. Remove and discard bay leaf. Combine some hot liquid from slow cooker with sour cream in small bowl. Add mixture to slow cooker; stir. Stir in bacon.

Makes 6 to 8 servings

Potato and Leek Soup

Vegetable Medley Soup

Slow Cooker Recipe

3 sweet potatoes, peeled and chopped
3 zucchini, chopped
2 cups chopped broccoli
1 onion, chopped
¼ cup butter, melted
3 cans (about 14 ounces each) chicken broth
2 white potatoes, peeled and shredded
1 rib celery, finely chopped
1 tablespoon salt
1 teaspoon ground cumin
1 teaspoon black pepper
2 cups half-and-half or milk

Combine sweet potatoes, zucchini, broccoli, onion and butter in large bowl. Add chicken broth; stir. Add white potatoes, celery, salt, cumin and pepper; stir. Pour mixture into slow cooker. Cover and cook on Low 8 to 10 hours or on High 4 to 5 hours. Add half-and-half; cook 30 minutes to 1 hour. *Makes 12 servings*

Food Fact: *As with conventional cooking recipes, slow cooker recipe time ranges are provided to account for variables such as temperature of ingredients before cooking, how full the slow cooker is and even altitude. Once you become familiar with your slow cooker, you'll have a good idea which end of the range to use.*

Vegetable Medley Soup

Swanson® Chicken Noodle Soup Express

2 cans (14½ ounces *each*) SWANSON® Chicken Broth
    Generous dash pepper
1 medium carrot, sliced (about ½ cup)
1 stalk celery, sliced (about ½ cup)
½ cup *uncooked* medium egg noodles
1 can (5 ounces) SWANSON® Premium Chunk Chicken Breast
    or Chunk Chicken, drained

In medium saucepan mix broth, pepper, carrot and celery. Over medium-high heat, heat to a boil. Stir in noodles. Reduce heat to medium. Cook 10 minutes, stirring often. Add chicken and heat through.   *Makes 4 servings*

Swanson® Easy Vegetable Soup

2 cans (14½ ounces *each*) SWANSON® Chicken Broth
3 cups CAMPBELL'S® Tomato Juice
1 teaspoon dried oregano leaves *or* Italian seasoning, crushed
½ teaspoon garlic powder *or* 4 cloves garlic, minced
¼ teaspoon pepper
1 bag (16 ounces) frozen vegetable combination (broccoli,
    cauliflower, carrots)
1 can (about 15 ounces) kidney beans *or* 1 can (about
    16 ounces) white kidney (cannellini) beans, rinsed and
    drained

In large saucepan mix broth, tomato juice, oregano, garlic powder, pepper and vegetables. Over medium-high heat, heat to a boil. Cover and cook 10 minutes or until vegetables are tender. Add beans and heat through.   *Makes 8 servings*

**Top to bottom: Swanson® Easy Vegetable Soup and
Swanson® Chicken Noodle Soup Express**

Tomato Chicken Gumbo

6 chicken thighs
½ pound hot sausage links or Polish sausage, sliced
3 cups water
1 can (14 ounces) chicken broth
½ cup uncooked long-grain white rice
1 can (26 ounces) DEL MONTE® Traditional or Chunky Garlic
   and Herb Spaghetti Sauce
1 can (11 ounces) DEL MONTE® SUMMER CRISP™ Whole
   Kernel Golden Sweet Corn, drained
1 medium green bell pepper, diced

1. Preheat oven to 400°F. In large shallow baking pan, place chicken and sausage. Bake 35 minutes or until chicken is no longer pink in center. Cool slightly.

2. Remove skin from chicken; cut meat into cubes. Cut sausage into slices ½ inch thick.

3. In 6-quart pot, bring water and broth to a boil. Add chicken, sausage and rice. Cover; cook over medium heat 15 minutes.

4. Stir in spaghetti sauce, corn and bell pepper; bring to a boil. Cover; cook 5 minutes or until rice is tender.   *Makes 4 servings*

Tip: Add additional water or broth for a thinner gumbo. For spicier gumbo, serve with hot red pepper sauce.

Tomato Chicken Gumbo

Slews of Stews

The Best Beef Stew

Slow Cooker Recipe

½ cup plus 2 tablespoons all-purpose flour, divided
2 teaspoons salt
1 teaspoon black pepper
3 pounds beef stew meat, trimmed and cut into cubes
1 can (16 ounces) diced tomatoes in juice, undrained
½ pound smoked sausage, sliced
3 potatoes, peeled and diced
1 cup chopped leek
1 cup chopped onion
4 ribs celery, sliced
½ cup chicken broth
3 cloves garlic, minced
1 teaspoon dried thyme leaves
3 tablespoons water

Combine ½ cup flour, salt and pepper in resealable plastic food storage bag. Add beef; shake bag to coat beef. Place beef in slow cooker. Add remaining ingredients except remaining 2 tablespoons flour and water; stir well. Cover and cook on Low 8 to 12 hours or on High 4 to 6 hours. One hour before serving, turn slow cooker to High. Combine remaining 2 tablespoons flour and water in small bowl. Stir mixture into slow cooker; mix well. Cover and cook until thickened.

Makes 8 servings

The Best Beef Stew

Turkey Mushroom Stew

Slow Cooker Recipe

1 pound turkey cutlets, cut into 4×1-inch strips
1 small yellow onion, thinly sliced
2 tablespoons minced green onions with tops
½ pound mushrooms, sliced
2 to 3 tablespoons flour
1 cup half-and-half or milk
1 teaspoon dried tarragon leaves
1 teaspoon salt
   Black pepper to taste
½ cup frozen peas
½ cup sour cream (optional)
   Puff pastry shells

Layer turkey, onions and mushrooms in slow cooker. Cover and cook on Low 4 hours. Remove turkey and vegetables to serving bowl. Turn slow cooker to High.

Blend flour into half-and-half until smooth; pour into slow cooker. Add tarragon, salt and pepper to slow cooker. Return cooked vegetables and turkey to slow cooker. Stir in peas. Cover and cook 1 hour or until sauce has thickened and peas are heated through.

Stir in sour cream just before serving, if desired. Serve in puff pastry shells.   *Makes 4 servings*

Turkey Mushroom Stew

Santa Fe Stew Olé

1 tablespoon vegetable oil
1½ pounds beef stew meat, cut into bite-size pieces
1 can (28 ounces) stewed tomatoes, undrained
2 medium carrots, cut into ¼-inch slices
1 medium onion, coarsely chopped
2 tablespoons diced green chiles
1 package (1.0 ounce) LAWRY'S® Taco Spices & Seasonings
½ teaspoon LAWRY'S® Seasoned Salt
¼ cup water
2 tablespoons all-purpose flour
1 can (15 ounces) pinto beans, drained

In Dutch oven, heat oil. Brown stew meat over medium-high heat. Add tomatoes, carrots, onion, green chiles, Taco Spices & Seasonings and Seasoned Salt; mix well. Bring to a boil over medium-high heat; reduce heat to low and cook, covered, 40 minutes. In small bowl, combine water and flour; mix well. Stir into stew mixture. Add pinto beans; cook over low heat 15 minutes. *Makes 4 servings*

Serving Suggestion: Serve with lots of warm corn and flour tortillas.

Santa Fe Stew Olé

Deviled Beef Short Rib Stew

4 pounds beef short ribs, trimmed
2 pounds small red potatoes, scrubbed
    and scored
8 carrots, peeled and cut into chunks
2 onions, cut into thick wedges
1 bottle (12 ounces) beer or non-alcoholic malt beverage
8 tablespoons FRENCH'S® Deli Brown Mustard, divided
3 tablespoons FRENCH'S® Worcestershire Sauce, divided
2 tablespoons cornstarch

1. Broil ribs 6 inches from heat on rack in broiler pan 10 minutes or until well-browned, turning once. Place potatoes, carrots and onions in bottom of slow cooker. Place ribs on top of vegetables.

2. Combine beer, *6 tablespoons* mustard and *2 tablespoons* Worcestershire. Pour into slow cooker. Cover and cook on high-heat setting 5 hours* or until meat is tender.

3. Transfer meat and vegetables to platter; keep warm. Strain fat from broth; pour into saucepan. Combine cornstarch with *2 tablespoons cold water.* Stir into broth with remaining *2 tablespoons* mustard and *1 tablespoon* Worcestershire. Heat to boiling. Reduce heat to medium-low. Cook 1 to 2 minutes or until thickened, stirring often. Pass gravy with meat and vegetables. Serve meat with additional mustard.   *Makes 6 servings (with 3 cups gravy)*

*Or cook 10 hours on low-heat setting.

Deviled Beef Short Rib Stew

98   Slews of Stews

Stew Provençal

2 cans (about 14 ounces each) beef broth, divided
⅓ cup all-purpose flour
1½ pounds pork tenderloin, trimmed and diced
4 red potatoes, unpeeled, cut into cubes
2 cups frozen cut green beans
1 onion, chopped
2 cloves garlic, minced
1 teaspoon salt
1 teaspoon dried thyme leaves
½ teaspoon black pepper

Combine ¾ cup beef broth and flour in small bowl. Set aside.

Add remaining broth, pork, potatoes, beans, onion, garlic, salt, thyme and pepper to slow cooker; stir. Cover and cook on Low 8 to 10 hours or on High 4 to 5 hours. If cooking on Low, turn to High last 30 minutes. Stir in flour mixture. Cook 30 minutes to thicken.

Makes 8 servings

Food Fact: *You can easily remove most of the fat from accumulated juices, soups and canned broths. The simplest way is to refrigerate the liquid for several hours or overnight. The fat will congeal and float to the top for easy removal.*

It's Chili Tonight

Bandstand Chili

---

1 tablespoon vegetable oil
1½ cups chopped onions
1½ cups chopped red bell peppers
2 tablespoons mild Mexican seasoning*
1 clove garlic, minced
1 can (28 ounces) tomato purée with tomato bits
1 can (15½ ounces) light red kidney beans, undrained
2 cups chopped cooked BUTTERBALL® Boneless Young Turkey

---

*To make your own Mexican seasoning, combine 1 tablespoon chili powder, 1½ teaspoons oregano and 1½ teaspoons cumin.

Heat oil in large skillet over medium heat until hot. Add onions, bell peppers, Mexican seasoning and garlic. Cook and stir 4 to 5 minutes. Add tomato purée and beans; stir in turkey. Reduce heat to low; simmer 5 minutes. *Makes 8 servings*

Bandstand Chili

Vegetable-Beef Chili

1 (1-pound) beef top round or chuck steak, cut into ¼-inch cubes
1 tablespoon vegetable oil
1 cup coarsely chopped green bell pepper
½ cup coarsely chopped onion
1 clove garlic, minced
3 to 4 tablespoons chili powder
2 (16-ounce) cans tomatoes, undrained, coarsely chopped
¾ cup A.1.® Original or A.1.® Bold & Spicy Steak Sauce
1 (17-ounce) can corn, drained
1 (15-ounce) can kidney beans, drained

In 6-quart pot, over medium-high heat, brown steak in oil; drain if necessary. Reduce heat to medium; add pepper, onion and garlic. Cook and stir until vegetables are tender, about 3 minutes. Mix in chili powder; cook and stir 1 minute. Add tomatoes with liquid and steak sauce; heat to a boil. Reduce heat. Cover; simmer 45 minutes, stirring occasionally. Add corn and beans; simmer 15 minutes or until steak is tender. Serve immediately. Garnish as desired.

Makes 6 servings

Vegetable-Beef Chili

Chili with Beans and Corn

Slow Cooker Recipe

1 (16-ounce) can black-eyed peas or
   cannellini beans, rinsed and drained
1 (16-ounce) can kidney or navy beans, rinsed
   and drained
1 (15-ounce) can whole tomatoes, drained and chopped
1 onion, chopped
1 cup corn
1 cup water
½ cup chopped green onions
½ cup tomato paste
¼ cup diced canned jalapeño peppers
1 tablespoon chili powder
1 teaspoon mustard
1 teaspoon ground cumin
½ teaspoon dried oregano leaves

Combine all ingredients in slow cooker. Cover and cook on Low 8 to
10 hours or on High 4 to 5 hours.   *Makes 6 to 8 servings*

Food Fact: *Keep a lid on it! The slow cooker can take as long as
twenty minutes to regain the heat lost when the cover is removed. If
the recipe calls for stirring or checking the dish near the end of the
cooking time, replace the lid as quickly as you can.*

Chili with Beans and Corn

Meaty Chili

1 pound coarsely ground beef
¼ pound ground Italian sausage
1 large onion, chopped
2 medium ribs celery, diced
2 fresh jalapeño peppers,* chopped
2 cloves garlic, minced
1 can (28 ounces) whole peeled tomatoes, undrained, cut up
1 can (15 ounces) pinto beans, drained
1 can (12 ounces) tomato juice
1 cup water
¼ cup ketchup
1 teaspoon sugar
1 teaspoon chili powder
½ teaspoon salt
½ teaspoon ground cumin
½ teaspoon dried thyme leaves
⅛ teaspoon black pepper

*Jalapeño peppers can sting and irritate the skin; wear rubber gloves when handling peppers and do not touch eyes.

Cook beef, sausage, onion, celery, jalapeños and garlic in 5-quart Dutch oven over medium-high heat until meat is browned and onion is tender, stirring frequently.

Stir in tomatoes with liquid, beans, tomato juice, water, ketchup, sugar, chili powder, salt, cumin, thyme and black pepper. Bring to a boil over high heat. Reduce heat to medium-low; simmer, uncovered, 30 minutes, stirring occasionally.

Ladle into bowls. Garnish, if desired.   *Makes 6 servings*

Meaty Chili

Main Dish Magic

Simple Coq au Vin

Slow Cooker Recipe

4 chicken legs
   Salt and black pepper
2 tablespoons olive oil
½ pound mushrooms, sliced
1 onion, sliced into rings
½ cup red wine
½ teaspoon dried basil leaves
½ teaspoon dried thyme leaves
½ teaspoon dried oregano leaves
   Hot cooked rice

Sprinkle chicken with salt and pepper. Heat oil in large skillet; brown chicken on both sides. Remove chicken and place in slow cooker. Sauté mushrooms and onion in same skillet. Add wine; stir and scrape brown bits from bottom of skillet. Add mixture to slow cooker. Sprinkle with basil, thyme and oregano. Cover and cook on Low 8 to 10 hours or on High 3 to 4 hours.

Serve chicken and sauce over rice. *Makes 4 servings*

Simple Coq au Vin

Stewed Catfish and Bell Peppers

1½ pounds catfish fillets or other firm white-fleshed fish
1 onion, chopped
1 *each* green and red bell pepper, cut into 1-inch pieces
1 clove garlic, minced
1 cup clam juice
1 tomato, chopped
¼ cup FRANK'S® REDHOT® Sauce
2 tablespoons minced parsley

1. On sheet of waxed paper, mix *2 tablespoons flour* with *½ teaspoon salt.* Lightly coat fillets with flour mixture; set aside.

2. Heat *1 tablespoon oil* in large nonstick skillet until hot. Add onion, bell peppers and garlic. Cook and stir 3 minutes or until crisp-tender; transfer to dish.

3. Heat *1 tablespoon oil* in same skillet until hot. Cook fillets 5 minutes or until golden brown, turning once. Return vegetables to skillet. Add clam juice, tomato, REDHOT sauce and parsley. Heat to boiling. Reduce heat to medium-low. Cook, covered, 8 to 10 minutes or until fish flakes with fork. Serve with hot cooked rice, if desired.

Makes 6 servings

Stewed Catfish and Bell Peppers

Barbara's Pork Chop Dinner

Slow Cooker Recipe

1 tablespoon butter
1 tablespoon olive oil
6 bone-in pork loin chops
1 can (10¾ ounces) condensed cream of chicken soup,
   undiluted
1 can (4 ounces) mushrooms, drained and chopped
¼ cup Dijon mustard
¼ cup chicken broth
2 cloves garlic, minced
½ teaspoon salt
½ teaspoon dried basil leaves
¼ teaspoon black pepper
6 red potatoes, unpeeled, cut into thin slices
1 onion, sliced
  Chopped parsley

Heat butter and oil in large skillet. Brown pork chops on both sides.
Set aside.

Combine soup, mushrooms, mustard, chicken broth, garlic, salt,
basil and pepper in slow cooker. Add potatoes and onion, stirring to
coat. Place pork chops on top of potato mixture. Cover and cook on
Low 8 to 10 hours or on High 4 to 5 hours. Sprinkle with parsley.

Makes 6 servings

Barbara's Pork Chop Dinner

Classic Cabbage Rolls

  6 cups water
12 large cabbage leaves
  1 pound lean ground lamb
½ cup cooked rice
  1 teaspoon salt
¼ teaspoon dried oregano leaves
¼ teaspoon ground nutmeg
¼ teaspoon black pepper
1½ cups tomato sauce

Bring water to a boil in large saucepan. Turn off heat. Soak cabbage leaves in water 5 minutes; remove, drain and cool.

Combine lamb, rice, salt, oregano, nutmeg and pepper in large bowl. Place 2 tablespoonfuls mixture in center of each cabbage leaf; roll firmly. Place cabbage rolls in slow cooker, seam-side down. Pour tomato sauce over cabbage rolls. Cover and cook on Low 8 to 10 hours. *Makes 6 servings*

Food Fact: *Once your dish is cooked, don't keep it in the slow cooker too long. Foods need to be kept cooler than 40°F or hotter than 140°F to avoid the growth of harmful bacteria. Remove food to a clean container, cover and refrigerate as soon as possible. Do not reheat leftovers in the slow cooker. Use a microwave oven, the range-top or the oven for reheating.*

Classic Cabbage Rolls

Spanish-Style Couscous

Slow Cooker Recipe

1 pound lean ground beef
1 can (about 14 ounces) beef broth
1 small green bell pepper, cut into ½-inch pieces
½ cup pimiento-stuffed green olives, sliced
½ medium onion, chopped
2 cloves garlic, minced
1 teaspoon ground cumin
½ teaspoon dried thyme leaves
1⅓ cups water
1 cup uncooked couscous

Heat skillet over high heat until hot. Add beef; cook until browned. Pour off fat. Place broth, bell pepper, olives, onion, garlic, cumin, thyme and beef in slow cooker. Cover and cook on Low 4 hours or until bell pepper is tender.

Bring water to a boil over high heat in small saucepan. Stir in couscous. Cover; remove from heat. Let stand 5 minutes; fluff with fork. Spoon couscous onto plates; top with beef mixture.

Makes 4 servings

Food Fact: *To clean your slow cooker, follow the manufacturer's instructions. To make cleanup even easier, spray with nonstick cooking spray before adding food.*

Spanish-Style Couscous

Turkey and Macaroni

Slow Cooker Recipe

   1 teaspoon vegetable oil
1½ pounds ground turkey
   2 cans (10¾ ounces each) condensed tomato soup, undiluted
   2 cups uncooked macaroni, cooked and drained
   1 can (16 ounces) corn, drained
½ cup chopped onion
   1 can (4 ounces) sliced mushrooms, drained
   2 tablespoons ketchup
   1 tablespoon mustard
      Salt and black pepper to taste

Heat oil in medium skillet; cook turkey until browned. Transfer mixture to slow cooker. Add remaining ingredients to slow cooker. Stir to blend. Cover and cook on Low 7 to 9 hours or on High 3 to 4 hours. *Makes 4 to 6 servings*

Food Fact: *Always taste the finished dish before serving to adjust seasonings to your preference. Consider adding a dash of the following: salt, pepper, seasoned salt, seasoned herb blends, lemon juice, soy sauce, Worcestershire sauce, flavored vinegar or minced fresh herbs.*

Turkey and Macaroni

Mile-High Enchilada Pie

Slow Cooker Recipe

5 (6-inch) corn tortillas
1 jar (12 ounces) prepared salsa
1 can (15½ ounces) kidney beans, rinsed and
    drained
1 cup shredded cooked chicken
1 cup shredded Monterey Jack with jalapeño cheese

Prepare foil handles for slow cooker (see below); place in slow cooker. Place 1 tortilla on bottom of slow cooker. Top with small amount of salsa, beans, chicken and cheese. Continue layering using remaining ingredients, ending with 1 tortilla and cheese. Cover and cook on Low 6 to 8 hours or on High 3 to 4 hours. Pull out by foil handles. *Makes 4 servings*

Foil Handles: Tear off three 18×2-inch strips of heavy foil or use regular foil folded to double thickness. Crisscross foil strips in spoke design and place in slow cooker to make lifting of tortilla stack easier.

Mile-High Enchilada Pie

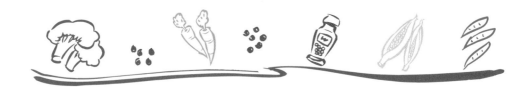

Beef Bourguignon

Slow Cooker Recipe

1 boneless beef sirloin steak, ½ inch thick, trimmed and cut into ½-inch pieces (about 3 pounds)
½ cup all-purpose flour
4 slices bacon, diced
2 medium carrots, diced
8 small new red potatoes, unpeeled, cut into quarters
8 to 10 mushrooms, sliced
20 to 24 pearl onions
3 cloves garlic, minced
1 bay leaf
1 teaspoon dried marjoram leaves
½ teaspoon dried thyme leaves
½ teaspoon salt
Black pepper to taste
2½ cups Burgundy wine or beef broth

Coat beef with flour, shaking off excess. Set aside.

Cook bacon in large skillet over medium heat until partially cooked. Add beef; cook until browned. Remove beef and bacon with slotted spoon.

Layer carrots, potatoes, mushrooms, onions, garlic, bay leaf, marjoram, thyme, salt, pepper, beef and bacon mixture and wine in slow cooker. Cover and cook on Low 8 to 9 hours or until beef is tender. Remove and discard bay leaf before serving.

Makes 10 to 12 servings

Beef Bourguignon

3-Cheese Chicken & Noodles

Slow Cooker Recipe

  3 cups chopped cooked chicken
1½ cups cottage cheese
  1 can (10¾ ounces) condensed cream of chicken soup,
      undiluted
  1 (8-ounce) package wide egg noodles, cooked and drained
  1 cup grated Monterey Jack cheese
  ½ cup chicken broth
  ½ cup diced celery
  ½ cup diced onion
  ½ cup diced green bell pepper
  ½ cup diced red bell pepper
  ½ cup grated Parmesan cheese
  1 can (4 ounces) sliced mushrooms, drained
  2 tablespoons butter, melted
  ½ teaspoon dried thyme leaves

Combine all ingredients in slow cooker. Stir to coat evenly. Cover and cook on Low 6 to 10 hours or on High 3 to 4 hours.

Makes 6 servings

Food Fact: *Vegetables often take longer to cook than meats. Cut vegetables into small, thin pieces and place them near the bottom or sides of the slow cooker. Pay careful attention to the recipe instructions in order to cut vegetables to the proper size so they will cook in the amount of time given.*

3-Cheese Chicken & Noodles

Steak San Marino

Slow Cooker Recipe

¼ cup all-purpose flour
1 teaspoon salt
½ teaspoon black pepper
4 beef round steaks, about 1 inch thick
1 can (8 ounces) tomato sauce
2 carrots, chopped
½ onion, chopped
1 rib celery, chopped
1 teaspoon dried Italian seasoning
½ teaspoon Worcestershire sauce
1 bay leaf
   Hot cooked rice

Combine flour, salt and pepper in small bowl. Dredge each steak in flour mixture. Place in slow cooker. Combine tomato sauce, carrots, onion, celery, Italian seasoning, Worcestershire sauce and bay leaf in small bowl; pour into slow cooker. Cover and cook on Low 8 to 10 hours or on High 4 to 5 hours.

Remove and discard bay leaf. Serve steaks and sauce over rice.

Makes 4 servings

Food Fact: *A good tip to keep in mind while shopping is that you can, and in fact should, use tougher, inexpensive cuts of meat. Top-quality cuts, such as loin chops or filet mignon, fall apart during long cooking periods and therefore are not great choices to use in the slow cooker. Keep those for roasting, broiling or grilling and save money when you use your slow cooker.*

Steak San Marino

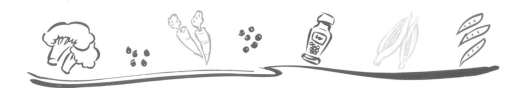

Pineapple Chicken and Sweet Potatoes

Slow Cooker Recipe

⅔ cup plus 3 tablespoons all-purpose flour, divided
1 teaspoon salt
1 teaspoon ground nutmeg
½ teaspoon ground cinnamon
⅛ teaspoon onion powder
⅛ teaspoon black pepper
6 chicken breasts
3 sweet potatoes, peeled and sliced
1 can (10¾ ounces) condensed cream of chicken soup, undiluted
½ cup pineapple juice
¼ pound mushrooms, sliced
2 teaspoons brown sugar
½ teaspoon grated orange peel
Hot cooked rice

Combine ⅔ cup flour, salt, nutmeg, cinnamon, onion powder and black pepper in large bowl. Thoroughly coat chicken in flour mixture. Place sweet potatoes on bottom of slow cooker. Top with chicken.

Combine soup, juice, mushrooms, remaining 3 tablespoons flour, sugar and orange peel in small bowl; stir well. Pour soup mixture into slow cooker. Cover and cook on Low 8 to 10 hours or on High 3 to 4 hours. Serve chicken and sauce over rice.

Makes 6 servings

Pineapple Chicken and Sweet Potatoes

Fiesta Rice and Sausage

Slow Cooker Recipe

1 teaspoon vegetable oil
2 pounds spicy Italian sausage, casing removed
2 cloves garlic, minced
2 teaspoons ground cumin
4 onions, chopped
4 green bell peppers, chopped
3 jalapeño peppers,* seeded and minced
4 cups beef broth
2 packages (6¼ ounces each) long-grain and wild rice mix

*Jalapeño peppers can sting and irritate the skin; wear rubber gloves when handling peppers and do not touch eyes.

Heat oil in large skillet; add sausage. Break up sausage with back of spoon while cooking; cook until browned, about 5 minutes. Add garlic and cumin; cook 30 seconds. Add onions, bell peppers and jalapeño peppers. Sauté mixture until onions are tender, about 10 minutes. Pour mixture into slow cooker. Stir in beef broth and rice.

Cover and cook on High 1 to 2 hours or on Low 4 to 6 hours.

Makes 10 to 12 servings

Food Fact: *If you do any advance preparation, such as trimming meat or cutting vegetables, make sure you then cover and refrigerate the food until you are ready to start cooking. Store uncooked meats and vegetables separately. If you are preparing meat, poultry or fish, remember to wash your cutting board, utensils and hands with soap and hot water before touching other foods.*

Fiesta Rice and Sausage

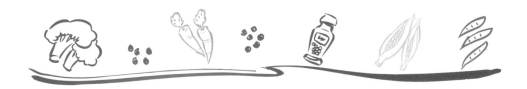

Mom's Tuna Casserole

Slow Cooker Recipe

2 cans (12 ounces each) tuna, drained and
   flaked
3 cups diced celery
3 cups crushed potato chips, divided
6 hard-cooked eggs, chopped
1 can (10¾ ounces) condensed cream of mushroom soup,
   undiluted
1 can (10¾ ounces) condensed cream of celery soup,
   undiluted
1 cup mayonnaise
1 teaspoon dried tarragon leaves
1 teaspoon black pepper

Combine all ingredients, except ½ cup potato chips, in slow cooker;
stir well. Top mixture with remaining ½ cup potato chips. Cover and
cook on Low 5 to 8 hours.   *Makes 8 servings*

Mom's Tuna Casserole

Cheesy Pork and Potatoes

½ pound ground pork, cooked and crumbled
½ cup finely crushed saltine crackers
⅓ cup barbecue sauce
1 egg
3 tablespoons margarine
1 tablespoon vegetable oil
4 potatoes, peeled and thinly sliced
1 onion, thinly sliced
1 cup grated mozzarella cheese
⅔ cup evaporated milk
1 teaspoon salt
¼ teaspoon paprika
⅛ teaspoon black pepper
    Chopped parsley

Slow Cooker Recipe

Combine pork, crackers, barbecue sauce and egg in large bowl; shape mixture into 6 patties. Heat margarine and oil in medium skillet. Sauté potatoes and onion until lightly browned. Drain and place in slow cooker.

Combine cheese, milk, salt, paprika and pepper in small bowl. Pour into slow cooker. Layer pork patties on top. Cover and cook on Low 3 to 5 hours. Garnish with parsley. *Makes 6 servings*

Food Fact: *The slow cooker can help you make lower-fat meals because you won't be cooking in fat as you do when you stir-fry and sauté. And tougher, inexpensive cuts of meat have less fat than prime cuts. Many recipes call for trimming excess fat from meat.*

Cheesy Pork and Potatoes

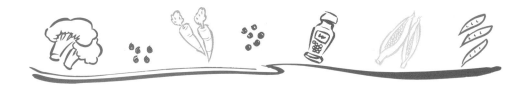

That's Italian Meat Loaf

Slow Cooker Recipe

1 (8-ounce) can tomato sauce, divided
1 egg, lightly beaten
½ cup chopped onion
½ cup chopped green bell pepper
⅓ cup dry seasoned bread crumbs
2 tablespoons grated Parmesan cheese
½ teaspoon garlic powder
¼ teaspoon black pepper
1 pound ground beef
½ pound ground pork or veal
1 cup shredded Asiago cheese

Reserve ⅓ cup tomato sauce; set aside in refrigerator. Combine remaining tomato sauce and egg in large bowl. Stir in onion, bell pepper, bread crumbs, Parmesan cheese, garlic powder and black pepper. Add ground beef and pork; mix well and shape into loaf.

Place meat loaf on foil handles (see page 276). Place in slow cooker. Cover and cook on Low 8 to 10 hours or on High 4 to 6 hours; internal temperature should read 170°F.

Spread meat loaf with reserved tomato sauce. Sprinkle with Asiago cheese. Cover and cook 15 minutes or until cheese is melted. Using foil handles, remove meat loaf from slow cooker.

Makes 8 servings

That's Italian Meat Loaf

Chicken Sausage Pilaf

1 tablespoon vegetable oil
1 pound chicken or turkey sausage, casing removed
1 cup uncooked rice and pasta mix
4 cups chicken broth
2 ribs celery, diced
¼ cup slivered almonds
Salt and black pepper to taste

Heat oil in large skillet; add sausage. Break up sausage with back of spoon while cooking; cook until browned, about 5 minutes. Add rice-pasta mix to skillet. Cook 1 minute. Place mixture in slow cooker. Add remaining ingredients to slow cooker; stir well. Cover and cook on Low 7 to 10 hours or on High 3 to 4 hours or until rice is tender.

Makes 4 servings

Food Fact: *If you do use fatty cuts of meat, such as sausage or ribs, consider browning them first on top of the range to cook off excess fat before adding them to the slow cooker.*

Chicken Sausage Pilaf

Classic Beef & Noodles

Slow Cooker Recipe

2 pounds beef stew meat, trimmed and cut
  into cubes
¼ pound mushrooms, sliced into halves
2 tablespoons chopped onion
2 cloves garlic, minced
1 teaspoon salt
1 teaspoon dried oregano leaves
½ teaspoon black pepper
¼ teaspoon dried marjoram leaves
1 bay leaf
1½ cups beef broth
⅓ cup dry sherry
1 (8-ounce) container sour cream
½ cup all-purpose flour
¼ cup water
4 cups hot cooked noodles

Combine beef, mushrooms, onion, garlic, salt, oregano, pepper, marjoram and bay leaf in slow cooker. Pour in beef broth and sherry. Cover and cook on Low 8 to 10 hours or on High 4 to 5 hours. Remove and discard bay leaf.

If cooking on Low, turn to High. Stir together sour cream, flour and water in small bowl. Stir about 1 cup liquid from slow cooker into sour cream mixture. Stir mixture back into slow cooker. Cover and cook on High 30 minutes or until thickened and bubbly. Serve over noodles.

Makes 8 servings

Classic Beef & Noodles

The Best of the Rest

Festive Bacon & Cheese Dip

Slow Cooker Recipe

2 packages (8 ounces each) cream cheese,
    softened, cut into cubes
4 cups shredded Colby-Jack cheese
1 cup half-and-half
2 tablespoons mustard
1 tablespoon chopped onion
2 teaspoons Worcestershire sauce
½ teaspoon salt
¼ teaspoon hot pepper sauce
1 pound bacon, cooked and crumbled

Place cream cheese, Colby-Jack cheese, half-and-half, mustard,
onion, Worcestershire sauce, salt and pepper sauce in slow cooker.
Cover and cook, stirring occasionally, on Low 1 hour or until cheese
melts. Stir in bacon; adjust seasonings. Serve with crusty bread or
fruit and vegetable dippers. *Makes about 1 quart*

Festive Bacon & Cheese Dip

Oriental Chicken Wings

Slow Cooker Recipe

32 pieces chicken wing drums and flats
1 cup chopped red onion
1 cup soy sauce
¾ cup brown sugar
¼ cup dry sherry
2 tablespoons chopped fresh ginger
2 cloves garlic, minced
Chopped chives

Broil chicken wings, about 5 minutes per side. Transfer chicken to slow cooker.

Stir together onion, soy sauce, brown sugar, sherry, ginger and garlic in large bowl. Add to slow cooker; stir to combine. Cover and cook on Low 5 to 6 hours or on High 2 to 3 hours. Sprinkle with chives.
Makes 32 appetizers

Food Fact: *Chicken skin tends to shrivel and curl in the slow cooker, so most recipes call for skinless chicken. If you use skin-on pieces, brown them before adding them to the slow cooker.*

Oriental Chicken Wings

Suzie's Sloppy Joes

3 pounds lean ground beef
1 cup chopped onion
3 cloves garlic, minced
1¼ cups ketchup
1 cup chopped red bell pepper
5 tablespoons Worcestershire sauce
4 tablespoons brown sugar
3 tablespoons vinegar
3 tablespoons mustard
2 teaspoons chili powder
    Hamburger buns

Brown ground beef, onion and garlic in large skillet. Drain excess fat.

Combine ketchup, bell pepper, Worcestershire sauce, brown sugar, vinegar, mustard and chili powder in slow cooker. Stir in beef mixture. Cover and cook on Low 6 to 8 hours. Spoon into hamburger buns.   *Makes 8 to 10 servings*

BBQ Pork Sandwiches

Slow Cooker Recipe

4 pounds boneless pork loin roast, fat
   trimmed
1 can (14½ ounces) beef broth
⅓ cup FRENCH'S® Worcestershire Sauce
⅓ cup FRANK'S® REDHOT® Sauce

Sauce
½ cup ketchup
½ cup molasses
¼ cup FRENCH'S® CLASSIC YELLOW® Mustard
¼ cup FRENCH'S® Worcestershire Sauce
2 tablespoons FRANK'S® REDHOT® Sauce

1. Place roast on bottom of slow cooker. Combine broth, *⅓ cup each* Worcestershire and REDHOT sauce. Pour over roast. Cover and cook on high-heat setting 5 hours* or until roast is tender.

2. Meanwhile, combine ingredients for sauce in large bowl; set aside.

3. Transfer roast to large cutting board. Discard liquid. Coarsely chop roast. Stir into reserved sauce. Spoon pork mixture on large rolls. Serve with deli potato salad, if desired.   *Makes 8 to 10 servings*

*Or cook 10 hours on low-heat setting.

BBQ Pork Sandwich

Spicy Beans Tex-Mex

Slow Cooker Recipe

⅓ cup lentils
1⅓ cups water
5 strips bacon
1 onion, chopped
1 can (16 ounces) pinto beans, undrained
1 can (16 ounces) red kidney beans, undrained
1 can (15 ounces) diced tomatoes, undrained
3 tablespoons ketchup
3 cloves garlic, minced
1 teaspoon chili powder
½ teaspoon ground cumin
¼ teaspoon red pepper flakes
1 bay leaf

Boil lentils in water 20 to 30 minutes in large saucepan; drain. In small skillet, cook bacon until crisp; remove, drain and crumble bacon. In same skillet, cook onion in bacon drippings until soft. Combine lentils, bacon, onion, beans, tomatoes, ketchup, garlic, chili powder, cumin, pepper flakes and bay leaf in slow cooker. Cook on High 3 to 4 hours.   *Makes 8 to 10 servings*

Spicy Beans Tex-Mex

Donna's Potato Casserole

Slow Cooker Recipe

1 can (10¾ ounces) condensed cream of
    chicken soup, undiluted
8 ounces sour cream
¼ cup chopped onion
¼ cup plus 3 tablespoons butter, melted, divided
1 teaspoon salt
2 pounds potatoes, peeled and chopped
2 cups shredded Cheddar cheese
1½ to 2 cups stuffing mix

Combine soup, sour cream, onion, ¼ cup butter and salt in small bowl.

Combine potatoes and cheese in slow cooker. Pour soup mixture into slow cooker; mix well. Sprinkle stuffing mix over potato mixture; drizzle with remaining 3 tablespoons butter. Cover and cook on Low 8 to 10 hours or on High 5 to 6 hours.   *Makes 8 to 10 servings*

Food Fact: *If you'd like to adapt your own favorite recipe to a slow cooker recipe, you'll need to follow a few guidelines. First, try to find a similar slow cooker recipe in this publication or your manufacturer's guide. Note the cooking times, liquid, quantity and size of meat and vegetable pieces. Because the slow cooker captures moisture, you will want to reduce the amount of liquid, often by as much as half. Add dairy products toward the end of the cooking time so they do not curdle.*

Donna's Potato Casserole

"Peachy Keen" Dessert Treat

Slow Cooker Recipe

1⅓ cups rolled old-fashioned oats
1 cup granulated sugar
1 cup packed brown sugar
⅔ cup buttermilk baking mix
2 teaspoons ground cinnamon
½ teaspoon ground nutmeg
2 pounds fresh peaches (about 8 medium), sliced

Stir together oats, sugars, baking mix, cinnamon and nutmeg in large bowl. Stir in peaches; mix until well blended. Pour mixture into slow cooker. Cover and cook on Low 4 to 6 hours.

Makes 8 to 12 servings

Food Fact: *The benefits of your slow cooker:*

• *No need for constant attention or frequent stirring*

• *No worry about burning or overcooking*

• *No sink full of pots and pans to scrub at the end of a long day*

• *Great for parties and buffets*

• *Keeps your kitchen cool by keeping your oven turned off*

• *Saves energy—cooking on the low setting uses less energy than most light bulbs*

"Peachy Keen" Dessert Treat

Decadent Chocolate Delight

Slow Cooker Recipe

1 package chocolate cake mix
8 ounces sour cream
1 cup chocolate chips
1 cup water
4 eggs
¾ cup vegetable oil
1 (4-serving-size) package chocolate-flavor instant pudding
   and pie filling mix

Lightly grease inside of slow cooker.

Combine all ingredients in large bowl. Pour into slow cooker. Cover and cook on Low 6 to 8 hours or on High 3 to 4 hours. Serve hot or warm with ice cream. *Makes 12 servings*

Decadent Chocolate Delight

Asparagus and Cheese Side Dish

Slow Cooker Recipe

1½ pounds fresh asparagus, trimmed
  2 cups crushed saltine crackers
  1 can (10¾ ounces) condensed cream of asparagus soup,
    undiluted
  1 can (10¾ ounces) condensed cream of chicken soup,
    undiluted
  ¼ pound American cheese, cut into cubes
  ⅔ cup slivered almonds
  1 egg

Combine all ingredients in large bowl; stir well. Pour into slow cooker. Cover and cook on High 3 to 3½ hours.

Makes 4 to 6 servings

Food Fact: *Manufacturers recommend that slow cookers should be one-half to three-quarters full for best results.*

Slow Cooker

RECIPES

Slow Cooker

RECIPES

SOUP'S ON

Rustic Vegetable Soup

1 jar (16 ounces) picante sauce
1 package (10 ounces) frozen mixed vegetables,
    thawed
1 package (10 ounces) frozen cut green beans,
    thawed
1 can (10 ounces) condensed beef broth, undiluted
1 to 2 baking potatoes, cut in ½-inch pieces
1 medium green bell pepper, chopped
½ teaspoon sugar
¼ cup finely chopped parsley

Combine all ingredients, except parsley, in slow cooker.
Cover and cook on LOW 8 hours or on HIGH 4 hours.
Stir in parsley; serve. *Makes 8 servings*

Farmhouse Ham and Vegetable Chowder

2 cans (10½ ounces each) cream of celery soup
2 cups diced cooked ham
1 package (10 ounces) frozen corn
1 large baking potato, cut in ½-inch pieces
1 medium red bell pepper, diced
½ teaspoon dried thyme leaves
2 cups small broccoli florets
½ cup milk

1. Combine all ingredients, except broccoli and milk in slow cooker; stir to blend. Cover and cook on LOW 6 to 8 hours or on HIGH 3 to 4 hours.

2. If cooking on LOW, turn to HIGH and stir in broccoli and milk. Cover and cook 15 minutes or until broccoli is crisp tender.   *Makes 6 servings*

Turkey-Tomato Soup

2 medium turkey thighs, boned, skinned and cut
    into 1-inch pieces
2 small white or red potatoes, cubed
1¾ cups fat-free reduced-sodium chicken broth
1½ cups frozen corn
1 cup chopped onion
1 cup water
1 can (8 ounces) no-salt-added tomato sauce
¼ cup tomato paste
2 tablespoons Dijon mustard
1 teaspoon hot pepper sauce
½ teaspoon sugar
½ teaspoon garlic powder
¼ cup finely chopped parsley

Combine all ingredients, except parsley, in slow cooker.
Cover and cook on LOW 9 to 10 hours. Stir in parsley;
serve. *Makes 6 servings*

HELPFUL HINT

Serve this soup with thickly sliced whole grain bread for a nutritious and hearty weeknight dinner.

White Bean And Green Chile Pepper Soup

2 cans (15 ounces each) Great Northern beans,
   rinsed and drained
1 cup finely chopped yellow onion
1 can (4½ ounces) diced green chilies
1 teaspoon ground cumin, divided
½ teaspoon garlic powder
1 can (14½ ounces) fat-free chicken broth
¼ cup chopped fresh cilantro leaves
1 tablespoon extra virgin olive oil
⅓ cup sour cream (optional)

1. Combine beans, onion, chilies, ½ teaspoon cumin and garlic powder in slow cooker. Cook on LOW 8 hours or on HIGH 4 hours.

2. Stir in cilantro, olive oil and remaining ½ teaspoon cumin. Garnish with sour cream, if desired.

Makes 5 Servings

HELPFUL HINT

You can make this dish vegetarian by replacing the chicken broth with vegetable broth.

Easy Italian Vegetable Soup

1 can (14½ ounces) diced tomatoes, undrained
1 can (10½ ounces) condensed beef broth, undiluted
1 package (8 ounces) sliced mushrooms
1 medium zucchini, thinly sliced
1 medium green bell pepper, chopped
1 medium yellow onion, chopped
⅓ cup dry red wine or beef broth
1½ tablespoons dried basil leaves
2½ teaspoons sugar
1 tablespoon extra virgin olive oil
½ teaspoon salt
1 cup (4 ounces) shredded Mozzarella cheese
   (optional)

1. Combine tomatoes, broth, mushrooms, zucchini, bell pepper, onion, wine, basil and sugar in slow cooker. Cook on LOW 8 hours or on HIGH 4 hours.

2. Stir oil and salt into soup. Garnish with cheese, if desired. *Makes 5 to 6 servings*

Easy Italian Vegetable Soup

Ham and Navy Bean Soup

        8 ounces dried navy beans, rinsed and drained
        6 cups water
        1 ham bone
        1 medium yellow onion, chopped
        2 celery stalks, finely chopped
        2 bay leaves
     1½ teaspoons dried tarragon leaves
     1½ teaspoons salt
        ¼ teaspoon black pepper

1. Place beans in large bowl; cover completely with water. Soak 6 to 8 hours or overnight. Drain beans; discard water.

2. Combine beans, water, ham bone, onion, celery, bay leaves and tarragon leaves in slow cooker. Cook on LOW 8 hours or on HIGH 4 hours. Discard ham bone and bay leaves; stir in salt and pepper.   *Makes 8 servings*

Double Thick Baked Potato-Cheese Soup

    2 pounds baking potatoes, peeled and cut into
        ½-inch cubes
    2 cans (10½ ounces each) cream of mushroom soup
 1½ cups finely chopped green onions, divided
    ¼ teaspoon garlic powder
    ⅛ teaspoon ground red pepper
 1½ cups (6 ounces) shredded sharp Cheddar cheese
    1 cup (8 ounces) sour cream
    1 cup milk
       Black pepper

1. Combine potatoes, soup, 1 cup green onions, garlic powder and red pepper in slow cooker. Cover and cook on LOW 8 hours or on HIGH 4 hours.

2. Add cheese, sour cream and milk; stir until cheese has completely melted. Cover and cook on HIGH an additional 10 minutes. Season to taste with black pepper. Garnish with remaining green onions.

Makes 7 Servings

Creamy Turkey Soup

2 cans (10½ ounces each) cream of chicken soup
2 cups chopped cooked turkey breast meat
1 package (8 ounces) sliced mushrooms
1 medium yellow onion, chopped
1 teaspoon rubbed sage *or* ½ teaspoon dried poultry
    seasoning
1 cup frozen peas, thawed
½ cup milk
1 jar (about 4 ounces) diced pimiento

1. Combine soup, turkey, mushrooms, onion and sage in slow cooker. Cook on LOW 8 hours or on HIGH 4 hours.

2. If cooking on LOW, turn to HIGH; stir in peas, milk and pimientos. Cook an additional 10 minutes or until heated through.

Makes 5 to 6 servings

Creamy Turkey Soup

Campfire Sausage and Potato Soup

1 can (15½ ounces) dark kidney beans, rinsed and
    drained
1 can (14½ ounces) diced tomatoes, undrained
1 can (10½ ounces) condensed beef broth, undiluted
8 ounces kielbasa sausage, cut lengthwise into
    halves, then crosswise into ½-inch pieces
1 large baking potato, cut into ½-inch cubes
1 medium green bell pepper, diced
1 medium onion, diced
1 teaspoon dried oregano leaves
½ teaspoon sugar
1 to 2 teaspoons ground cumin

Combine all ingredients, except cumin, in slow cooker.
Cover and cook on LOW 8 hours or on HIGH 4 hours.
Stir in cumin; serve.   *Makes 6 to 7 servings*

HELPFUL HINT

Kielbasa sausage, also referred to as Polish sausage, is sold both fresh and in precooked links near the deli aisle.

*Campfire Sausage and
Potato Soup*

MAIN-DISH MAGIC

Caribbean Shrimp with Rice

   1 package (12 ounces) frozen shrimp, thawed
½ cup chicken broth
   1 clove garlic, minced
   1 teaspoon chili powder
½ teaspoon salt
½ teaspoon dried oregano leaves
   1 cup frozen peas
½ cup diced tomatoes
   2 cups cooked rice

Combine shrimp, broth, garlic, chili powder, salt and oregano in slow cooker. Cover and cook on LOW 2 hours. Add peas and tomatoes. Cover and cook on LOW 5 minutes. Stir in rice. Cover and cook on LOW an additional 5 minutes. *Makes 4 servings*

Turkey Breast with Barley-Cranberry Stuffing

2 cups fat-free reduced-sodium chicken broth

1 cup quick-cooking barley

½ cup chopped onion

½ cup dried cranberries

2 tablespoons slivered almonds, toasted

½ teaspoon rubbed sage

½ teaspoon garlic-pepper seasoning

Nonstick cooking spray

1 fresh or frozen bone-in turkey breast half (1¾- to 2-pound), thawed and skinned

⅓ cup finely chopped parsley

1. Combine broth, barley, onion, cranberries, almonds, sage and garlic-pepper seasoning in slow cooker.

2. Spray large nonstick skillet with cooking spray. Heat over medium heat until hot. Brown turkey breast on all sides; add to slow cooker. Cover and cook on LOW 3 to 4 hours or until internal temperature reaches 170°F when tested with meat thermometer inserted into the thickest part of breast, not touching bone.

3. Transfer turkey to cutting board; cover with foil and let stand 10 to 15 minutes before carving. Internal temperature will rise 5° to 10°F during stand time. Stir parsley into sauce mixture in slow cooker. Spoon sauce over turkey. *Makes 6 servings*

Cajun Sausage and Rice

8 ounces kielbasa sausage, cut in ¼-inch slices
1 can (14½ ounces) diced tomatoes, undrained
1 medium onion, diced
1 medium green bell pepper, diced
2 celery stalks, thinly sliced
1 tablespoon chicken bouillon granules
1 tablespoon steak sauce
3 bay leaves *or* 1 teaspoon dried thyme leaves
1 teaspoon sugar
¼ to ½ teaspoon hot pepper sauce
1 cup uncooked instant rice
½ cup chopped parsley (optional)

1. Combine sausage, tomatoes, onion, pepper, celery, bouillon, steak sauce, bay leaves, sugar and hot pepper sauce in slow cooker. Cover and cook on LOW 8 hours or on HIGH 4 hours.

2. Remove bay leaves; stir in rice and ½ cup water. Cook an additional 25 minutes. Stir in parsley, if desired.

Makes 5 servings

Shredded Pork Wraps

1 cup salsa, divided
2 tablespoons cornstarch
1 bone-in pork sirloin roast (2 pounds)
6 (8-inch) flour tortillas
⅓ cup shredded reduced-fat Cheddar cheese
3 cups broccoli slaw mix

1. Combine ¼ cup salsa and cornstarch in small bowl; stir until smooth. Pour mixture into slow cooker. Top with pork roast. Pour remaining ¾ cup salsa over roast.

2. Cover and cook on LOW 6 to 8 hours or until internal temperature reaches 165°F when tested with meat thermometer inserted into the thickest part of roast, not touching bone. Remove roast from slow cooker. Transfer roast to cutting board; cover with foil and let stand 10 to 15 minutes or until cool enough to handle before shredding. Internal temperature will rise 5° to 10°F during stand time. Trim and discard outer fat from pork. Using 2 forks, pull pork into coarse shreds.

3. Divide shredded meat evenly on each tortilla. Spoon about 2 tablespoons salsa mixture on top of meat in each tortilla. Top evenly with cheese and broccoli slaw mix. Fold bottom edge of tortilla over filling; fold in sides. Roll up completely to enclose filling. Repeat with remaining tortillas. Serve remaining salsa mixture as a dipping sauce. *Makes 6 servings*

Shredded Pork Wrap

Corned Beef and Cabbage

1 head cabbage (1½ pounds), cut into 6 wedges
4 ounces baby carrots
1 corned beef (3-pounds) with seasoning packet*
⅓ cup prepared mustard (optional)
⅓ cup honey (optional)

*If seasoning packet is not perforated, poke several small holes with tip of paring knife.

1. Place cabbage in slow cooker; top with carrots.

2. Place seasoning packet on top of vegetables. Place corned beef fat side up over seasoning packet and vegetables. Add 1 quart water. Cover and cook on LOW 10 hours.

3. Discard seasoning packet. Just before serving, combine mustard and honey in small bowl. Use as dipping sauce, if desired.   *Makes 6 servings*

Corned Beef and Cabbage

Chicken Teriyaki

  1 **pound boneless skinless chicken tenders**
  1 **can (6 ounces) pineapple juice**
¼ **cup soy sauce**
  1 **tablespoon sugar**
  1 **tablespoon minced fresh ginger**
  1 **tablespoon minced garlic**
  1 **tablespoon vegetable oil**
  1 **tablespoon molasses**
24 **cherry tomatoes (optional)**
  2 **cups hot cooked rice**

Combine all ingredients, except rice, in slow cooker.
Cover and cook on LOW 2 hours. Serve chicken and
sauce over rice.   *Makes 4 servings*

HELPFUL HINT

Chicken "tenders" or "supremes" are lean, tender strips found on the underside of the breast.

Southwestern Turkey in Chilies and Cream

1 boneless skinless turkey breast, cut into 1-inch pieces
2 tablespoons plus 2 teaspoons flour, divided
1 can (15 ounces) corn, well drained
1 can (4 ounces) diced green chilies, well drained
1 tablespoon butter
½ cup chicken broth
1 clove garlic, minced
1 teaspoon salt
½ teaspoon paprika
¼ teaspoon dried oregano leaves
¼ teaspoon black pepper
½ cup heavy cream
2 tablespoons chopped cilantro
3 cups hot cooked rice or pasta

1. Coat turkey pieces with 2 tablespoons flour; set aside. Place corn and green chilies in slow cooker.

2. Melt butter in large nonstick skillet over medium heat. Add turkey pieces; cook and stir 5 minutes or until lightly browned. Place turkey in slow cooker. Add broth, garlic, salt, paprika, oregano and pepper. Cover and cook on LOW 2 hours.

3. Stir cream and remaining 2 teaspoons flour in small bowl until smooth. Pour mixture into slow cooker. Cover and cook on HIGH 10 minutes or until slightly thickened. Stir in cilantro. Serve over rice.

Makes 6 (1½-cups) servings

Broccoli & Cheese Strata

    2 cups chopped broccoli florets
    4 slices firm white bread, ½-inch thick
    4 teaspoons butter
1½ cups (6 ounces) shredded Cheddar cheese
    3 eggs
1½ cups reduced-fat (2%) milk
    ½ teaspoon salt
    ½ teaspoon hot pepper sauce
    ⅛ teaspoon black pepper

1. Cook broccoli in boiling water 10 minutes or until tender. Drain. Spread one side of each bread slice with 1 teaspoon butter.

2. Arrange 2 slices bread, buttered sides up in greased 1-quart casserole. Layer cheese, broccoli and remaining 2 bread slices, buttered sides down.

3. Beat together eggs, milk, salt, hot pepper sauce and pepper in medium bowl. Gradually pour over bread.

4. Place small wire rack in 5-quart slow cooker. Pour in 1 cup water. Place casserole on rack. Cover and cook on HIGH 3 hours. *Makes 4 servings*

Broccoli & Cheese Strata

Beef and Vegetables in Rich Burgundy Sauce

1 package (8 ounces) sliced mushrooms
1 package (8 ounces) baby carrots
1 medium green bell pepper, cut into thin strips
1 boneless chuck roast (2½ pounds)
1 can (10½ ounces) golden mushroom soup
¼ cup dry red wine or beef broth
1 tablespoon Worcestershire sauce
1 package (1 ounce) dried onion soup mix
¼ teaspoon black pepper
2 tablespoons water
3 tablespoons cornstarch
4 cups hot cooked noodles
Chopped fresh parsley (optional)

1. Place mushrooms, carrots and bell pepper in slow cooker. Place roast on top of vegetables. Combine soup, wine, Worcestershire sauce, soup mix and black pepper in medium bowl; mix well. Pour soup mixture over roast. Cover and cook on LOW 8 to 10 hours.

2. Blend water into cornstarch in cup until smooth; set aside. Transfer roast to cutting board; cover with foil. Let stand 10 to 15 minutes before slicing.

3. Turn slow cooker to HIGH. Stir cornstarch mixture into vegetable mixture; cover and cook 10 minutes or until thickened. Serve over cooked noodles. Garnish with parsley, if desired.   *Makes 6 to 8 servings*

Beef and Vegetables in Rich Burgundy Sauce

Country Captain Chicken

4 chicken thighs
2 tablespoons all-purpose flour
2 tablespoons vegetable oil, divided
1 cup chopped green bell pepper
1 large onion, chopped
1 celery stalk, chopped
1 clove garlic, minced
¼ cup chicken broth
2 cups canned or fresh crushed tomatoes
½ cup golden raisins
1½ teaspoons curry powder
1 teaspoon salt
¼ teaspoon paprika
¼ teaspoon black pepper
2 cups hot cooked rice

1. Coat chicken with flour; set aside. Heat 1 tablespoon oil in large skillet over medium-high heat until hot. Add bell pepper, onion, celery and garlic. Cook and stir 5 minutes or until vegetables are tender. Place vegetables in slow cooker.

2. Heat remaining tablespoon oil in same skillet over medium-high heat. Add chicken and cook 5 minutes per side. Place chicken in slow cooker.

3. Pour broth into skillet. Heat over medium-high heat, stirring frequently and scraping up any browned bits from bottom of skillet. Pour liquid into slow cooker. Add tomatoes, raisins, curry powder, salt, paprika and pepper. Cover and cook on LOW 3 hours. Serve chicken with sauce over rice. *Makes 4 servings*

Mama Mia Spaghetti Sauce

        1 tablespoon olive oil
        1 package (8 ounces) sliced mushrooms
    ½ cup finely chopped carrots
        1 clove garlic, minced
        1 shallot, minced
        1 pound lean ground beef
        2 cups canned or fresh crushed tomatoes
    ½ cup dry red wine or beef broth
        2 tablespoons tomato paste
        1 teaspoon salt
        1 teaspoon dried oregano leaves
    ½ teaspoon dried basil leaves
    ¼ teaspoon black pepper
        4 cups cooked spaghetti
        Grated Parmesan cheese (optional)

1. Heat oil in large skillet over medium-high heat until hot. Add mushrooms, carrots, garlic and shallot to skillet. Cook and stir 5 minutes.

2. Place vegetables in slow cooker. Stir in ground beef crumbling it with spoon. Stir in tomatoes, wine, tomato paste, salt, oregano, basil and pepper. Cover and cook on HIGH 3 to 4 hours. Serve sauce with cooked spaghetti. Sprinkle with Parmesan cheese, if desired.

Makes 5 servings

De-Lite-Ful Dinners

& Desserts

Sweet Chicken Curry

  1 pound boneless skinless chicken breast, cut into
      1-inch pieces
  1 large green or red bell pepper, cut into 1-inch
      pieces
  1 large onion, sliced
  1 large tomato, seeded and chopped
  ½ cup mango chutney
  2 tablespoons cornstarch
1½ teaspoons curry powder
1⅓ cups hot cooked rice

1. Place chicken, bell pepper and onion in slow cooker. Top with tomato. Mix chutney, ¼ cup water, cornstarch and curry powder in large bowl.

continued on page 194

192

Sweet Curry Chicken, *continued*

2. Pour chutney mixture over chicken mixture in slow cooker. Cover and cook on LOW 3½ to 4½ hours. Serve over rice. *Makes 4 servings*

Nutrients per serving: *Calories: 326, Calories from Fat: 9%, Protein: 28 g, Carbohydrate: 45 g, Cholesterol: 69 mg, Sodium: 73 mg, Fiber: 3 g*
DIETARY EXCHANGES: *1 Vegetable, 1 Fruit, 1 Starch, 3 Lean Meat*

Hungarian Lamb Goulash

1 package (16 ounces) frozen cut green beans
1 cup chopped onion
1¼ pounds lean lamb stew meat, cut into 1-inch pieces
1 can (15 ounces) chunky tomato sauce
1¾ cups reduced-sodium chicken broth
1 can (6 ounces) tomato paste
4 teaspoons paprika
3 cups hot cooked noodles

Place green beans and onion in slow cooker. Top with lamb. Combine remaining ingredients, except noodles in large bowl; mix well. Pour over lamb mixture. Cover and cook on LOW 6 to 8 hours. Stir. Serve over noodles. *Makes 6 servings*

Nutrients per serving: *Calories: 289, Calories from Fat: 16%, Protein: 22 g, Carbohydrate: 39 g, Cholesterol: 67 mg, Sodium: 772 mg, Fiber: 7 g*
DIETARY EXCHANGES: *2 Vegetable, 2 Starch, 2 Lean Meat*

Orange Teriyaki Pork

    Nonstick cooking spray
 1 pound lean pork stew meat, cut into 1-inch cubes
 1 package (16 ounces) frozen pepper blend for
     stir-fry
 4 ounces sliced water chestnuts
 ½ cup orange juice
 2 tablespoons quick-cooking tapioca
 2 tablespoons brown sugar
 2 tablespoons teriyaki sauce
 ½ teaspoon ground ginger
 ½ teaspoon dry mustard
 1⅓ cups hot cooked rice

1. Spray large nonstick skillet with cooking spray; heat over medium heat until hot. Add pork; brown on all sides. Remove from heat; set aside.

2. Place peppers and water chestnuts in slow cooker. Top with browned pork. Mix orange juice, tapioca, brown sugar, teriyaki sauce, ginger and mustard in large bowl. Pour over pork mixture in slow cooker. Cover and cook on LOW 3 to 4 hours. Stir. Serve over rice.

Makes 4 servings

Nutrients per serving: *Calories: 313, Calories from Fat: 18%, Protein: 21 g, Carbohydrate: 42 g, Cholesterol: 49 mg, Sodium: 406 mg, Fiber: 4 g*
DIETARY EXCHANGES: *2 Vegetable, 2 Starch, 2 Lean Meat*

Hearty Lentil Stew

1 cup dried lentils, rinsed and drained
1 package (16 ounces) frozen green beans
2 cups cauliflower florets
1 cup chopped onion
1 cup baby carrots, cut in half crosswise
3 cups fat free reduced-sodium chicken broth
2 teaspoons ground cumin
¾ teaspoon ground ginger
1 can (15 ounces) chunky tomato sauce with garlic
    and herbs
½ cup dry-roasted peanuts

1. Place lentils in slow cooker. Top with green beans, cauliflower, onion and carrots. Combine broth, cumin and ginger in large bowl; mix well. Pour mixture over vegetables. Cover and cook on LOW 9 to 11 hours.

2. Stir in tomato sauce. Cover and cook on LOW 10 minutes. Ladle stew into bowls. Sprinkle peanuts evenly onto each serving.   *Makes 6 servings*

Nutrients per serving: *Calories: 264, Calories from Fat: 22%, Protein: 19 g, Carbohydrate: 35 g, Cholesterol: 0 mg, Sodium: 667 mg, Fiber: 16 g*
DIETARY EXCHANGES: *1 Vegetable, 2 Starch, 1 Lean Meat, 1 Fat*

Hearty Lentil Stew

Pork and Mushroom Ragout

Nonstick cooking spray
1 boneless pork loin roast (1¼ pounds)
1¼ cups canned crushed tomatoes, divided
2 tablespoons cornstarch
2 teaspoons dried savory leaves
3 sun-dried tomatoes, patted dry and chopped
1 package (8 ounces) sliced mushrooms
1 large onion, sliced
1 teaspoon black pepper
3 cups hot cooked noodles

1. Spray large nonstick skillet with cooking spray; heat over medium heat until hot. Brown roast on all sides; set aside.

2. Combine ½ cup crushed tomatoes, cornstarch, savory and sun-dried tomatoes in large bowl. Pour mixture into slow cooker. Layer mushrooms, onion and roast over tomato mixture.

3. Pour remaining tomatoes over roast; sprinkle with pepper. Cover and cook on LOW 4 to 6 hours or until internal temperature reaches 165°F when tested with meat thermometer inserted into the thickest part of roast.

continued on page 200

Pork and Mushroom Ragout

Pork and Mushroom Ragout, *continued*

4. Remove roast from slow cooker. Transfer roast to cutting board; cover with foil. Let stand 10 to 15 minutes before slicing. Internal temperature will continue to rise 5° to 10°F during stand time. Serve over hot cooked noodles.   *Makes 6 servings.*

Nutrients per serving: *Calories: 275, Calories from Fat: 22%, Protein: 21 g, Carbohydrate: 33 g, Cholesterol: 68 mg, Sodium: 169 mg, Fiber: 3 g*
DIETARY EXCHANGES: *1 Vegetable, 2 Starch, 2 Lean Meat*

Sweet Jalapeño Mustard Turkey Thighs

   3 turkey thighs, skin removed
   ¾ cup honey mustard
   ½ cup orange juice
   1 tablespoon cider vinegar
   1 teaspoon Worcestershire sauce
   1 to 2 jalapeño peppers, finely chopped
   1 clove garlic, minced
   ½ teaspoon grated orange peel

Place turkey thighs in single layer in slow cooker. Combine remaining ingredients in large bowl. Pour mixture over turkey thighs. Cover and cook on LOW 5 to 6 hours.   *Makes 6 servings*

Nutrients per serving: Calories: 157, Calories from Fat: 22%, Protein: 14 g, Carbohydrate: 14 g, Cholesterol: 40 mg, Sodium: 92 mg, Fiber: 1 g
DIETARY EXCHANGES: 1 Fruit, 1 Lean Meat

Irish Stew

1 cup fat-free reduced-sodium chicken broth

1 teaspoon dried marjoram leaves

1 teaspoon dried parsley leaves

¾ teaspoon salt

½ teaspoon garlic powder

¼ teaspoon black pepper

1¼ pounds white potatoes, peeled and cut into 1-inch pieces

1 pound lean lamb stew meat, cut into 1-inch cubes

8 ounces frozen cut green beans

2 small leeks, cut lengthwise into halves then crosswise into slices

1½ cups coarsely chopped carrots

Combine broth, marjoram, parsley, salt, garlic powder and pepper in large bowl; mix well. Pour mixture into slow cooker. Add potatoes, lamb, green beans, leeks and carrots. Cover and cook on LOW for 7 to 9 hours.

Makes 6 servings

Nutrients per serving: *Calories: 256, Calories from Fat: 20%, Protein: 20 g, Carbohydrate: 32 g, Cholesterol: 52 mg, Sodium: 388 mg, Fiber: 5 g*
DIETARY EXCHANGES: *2 Vegetable, 2 Starch, 2 Lean Meat*

Mu Shu Turkey

1 can (16 ounces) plums, drained, rinsed and pitted
½ cup orange juice
¼ cup finely chopped onion
1 tablespoon minced fresh ginger
¼ teaspoon ground cinnamon
1 pound boneless turkey breast, cut into thin strips
6 (7-inch) flour tortillas
3 cups coleslaw mix

1. Place plums in blender or food processor. Cover and blend until almost smooth. Combine plums, orange juice, onion, ginger and cinnamon in slow cooker; mix well. Place turkey strips over plum mixture. Cover and cook on LOW 3 to 4 hours.

2. Remove turkey strips from slow cooker and divide evenly among the tortillas. Spoon about 2 tablespoons plum sauce over turkey. Top evenly with coleslaw mix. Fold bottom edge of tortilla over filling; fold in sides. Roll up to completely enclose filling. Repeat with remaining tortillas. Use remaining plum sauce for dipping. *Makes 6 servings*

Nutrients per serving: *Calories: 248, Calories from Fat: 14%, Protein: 17 g, Carbohydrate: 36 g, Cholesterol: 30 mg, Sodium: 282 mg, Fiber: 3 g*
DIETARY EXCHANGES: *1 Vegetable, 1 Fruit, 1 Starch, 2 Lean Meat*

Mu Shu Turkey

Sauerbraten

    1 boneless, beef sirloin tip roast (1¼ pounds)
    3 cups baby carrots
1½ cups fresh or frozen pearl onions
  ¼ cup raisins
  ½ cup water
  ½ cup red wine vinegar
   1 tablespoon honey
  ½ teaspoon salt
  ½ teaspoon dry mustard
  ½ teaspoon garlic-pepper seasoning
  ¼ teaspoon ground cloves
  ¼ cup crushed crisp gingersnap cookies (5 cookies)

1. Heat large nonstick skillet over medium heat until hot. Brown roast on all sides; set aside.

2. Place roast, carrots, onions and raisins in slow cooker. Combine water, vinegar, honey, salt, mustard, garlic-pepper seasoning and cloves in large bowl; mix well. Pour mixture over meat and vegetables.

3. Cover and cook on LOW 4 to 6 hours or until internal temperature reaches 145°F when tested with meat thermometer inserted into thickest part of roast. Transfer roast to cutting board; cover with foil. Let stand 10 to 15 minutes before slicing. Internal temperature will continue to rise 5° to 10°F during stand time.

continued on page 206

Sauerbraten

Sauerbraten, *continued*

4. Remove vegetables with slotted spoon to bowl; cover to keep warm. Stir crushed cookies into sauce mixture in slow cooker. Cover and cook on HIGH 10 to 15 minutes or until sauce thickens. Serve meat and vegetables with sauce.   Makes 5 servings

Nutrients per serving: *Calories: 296, Calories from Fat: 26%, Protein: 28 g, Carbohydrate: 25 g, Cholesterol: 57 mg, Sodium: 381 mg, Fiber: 4 g*
DIETARY EXCHANGES: *3 Vegetable, 1 Fruit, 1 Starch, 3 Lean Meat*

Pear Crunch

    1 can (8 ounces) crushed pineapple in juice,
        undrained
   ¼ cup pineapple or apple juice
    3 tablespoons dried cranberries
  1½ teaspoons quick-cooking tapioca
   ¼ teaspoon vanilla extract
    2 pears, cored and cut into halves
   ¼ cup granola with almonds

Combine all ingredients, except pears and granola, in slow cooker; mix well. Place pears, cut side down, over pineapple mixture. Cover and cook on LOW 3½ to 4½ hours. Arrange pear halves on serving plates. Spoon pineapple mixture over pear halves. Garnish with granola.   .   *Makes 4 servings*

Nutrients per serving: *Calories: 133, Calories from Fat: 2%, Protein: 1 g, Carbohydrate: 34 g, Cholesterol: 0 mg, Sodium: 3 mg, Fiber: 3 g*
DIETARY EXCHANGES: *2 Fruit*

Pumpkin Custard

    2 eggs, beaten
    1 cup canned pumpkin
    ½ cup packed brown sugar
    ½ teaspoon ground ginger
    ½ teaspoon ground cinnamon
    ½ teaspoon grated lemon peel
    1 can (12 ounces) evaporated milk
      Additional ground cinnamon

1. Combine eggs, pumpkin, brown sugar, ginger, cinnamon and lemon peel in large bowl. Stir in evaporated milk. Pour mixture into a 1½-quart soufflé dish. Cover tightly with foil.

2. Make foil handles (see page 276). Place soufflé dish in slow cooker. Pour water into slow cooker to come about 1½ inches from top of soufflé dish. Cover and cook on LOW 4 hours.

3. Use foil handles to lift dish from slow cooker. Sprinkle with additional ground cinnamon. Serve warm.

Makes 6 servings

Nutrients per serving: *Calories: 256, Calories from Fat: 20%, Protein: 20 g, Carbohydrate: 32 g, Cholesterol: 52 mg, Sodium: 388 mg, Fiber: 5 g*
DIETARY EXCHANGES: *2 Vegetable, 2 Starch, 2 Lean Meat*

Luscious Pecan Bread Pudding

    3 cups French bread cubes
    3 tablespoons Chopped pecans, toasted
2¼ cups low-fat milk
    2 eggs, beaten
    ½ cup sugar
    1 teaspoon vanilla
    ¾ teaspoon ground cinnamon, divided
    ¾ cup reduced-calorie cranberry juice cocktail
1½ cups frozen pitted tart cherries
    2 tablespoons sugar substitute

1. Toss bread cubes and pecans in soufflé dish. Combine milk, eggs, sugar, vanilla and ½ teaspoon cinnamon in large bowl. Pour over bread mixture in soufflé dish. Cover tightly with foil. Make foil handles (see page 276). Place soufflé dish in slow cooker. Pour hot water into slow cooker to come about 1½ inches from top of soufflé dish. Cover and cook on LOW 2 to 3 hours.

2. Meanwhile, stir together cranberry juice and remaining ¼ teaspoon cinnamon in small saucepan; stir in frozen cherries. Bring sauce to boil over medium heat, about 5 minutes. Remove from heat. Stir in sugar substitute. Lift dish from slow cooker with foil handles. Serve with cherry sauce. *Makes 6 servings*

Nutrients per serving: *Calories: 238, Calories from Fat: 25%, Protein: 8 g, Carbohydrate: 38 g, Cholesterol: 78 mg, Sodium: 154 mg, Fiber: 2 g*
DIETARY EXCHANGES: *1 Fruit, 1 Starch, 1 Fat*

Luscious Pecan Bread Pudding

HEARTY STEWS

Panama Pork Stew

2 small sweet potatoes, peeled and cut into 2-inch
   pieces (about 12 ounces total)
1 package (10 ounces) frozen corn
1 package (9 ounces) frozen cut green beans
1 cup chopped onion
1¼ pounds lean pork stew meat, cut into 1-inch cubes
1 can (14½ ounces) diced tomatoes
1 to 2 tablespoons chili powder
½ teaspoon salt
½ teaspoon ground coriander

Place potatoes, corn, green beans and onion in slow
cooker. Top with pork. Stir together tomatoes, 1 cup
water, chili powder, salt and coriander in large bowl.
Pour over pork in slow cooker. Cover and cook on LOW
7 to 9 hours.   *Makes 6 servings*

Old World Chicken and Vegetables

1 tablespoon dried oregano leaves
1 teaspoon salt, divided
1 teaspoon paprika
½ teaspoon garlic powder
¼ teaspoon black pepper
2 medium green bell peppers, cut into thin strips
1 small yellow onion, thinly sliced
1 cut-up whole chicken (3 pounds)
⅓ cup ketchup
6 ounces dried uncooked egg noodles

1. In a small bowl, combine oregano, ½ teaspoon salt, paprika, garlic powder and pepper; mix well.

2. Place bell peppers and onion in slow cooker. Top with chicken thighs and legs, sprinkle with half of the oregano mixture, top with chicken breasts. Sprinkle chicken with remaining oregano mixture. Cover and cook on LOW 8 hours or on HIGH 4 hours. Stir in ketchup and ½ teaspoon salt. Just before serving, cook noodles following package directions; drain. Serve chicken pieces and vegetables over noodles.

Makes 4 servings

Middle Eastern Lamb Stew

1½ pounds lamb stew meat, cubed
2 tablespoons all-purpose flour
1 tablespoon vegetable oil
1½ cups beef broth
1 cup chopped onion
½ cup chopped carrots
1 clove garlic, minced
1 tablespoon tomato paste
½ teaspoon ground cumin
½ teaspoon red pepper flakes
¼ teaspoon ground cinnamon
½ cup chopped dried apricots
1 teaspoon salt
¼ teaspoon black pepper
3 cups hot cooked noodles

1. Coat lamb cubes with flour; set aside. Heat oil in large nonstick skillet over medium-high heat until hot. Brown half of lamb and transfer to slow cooker; repeat with remaining lamb. Add broth, onion, carrots, garlic, tomato paste, cumin, red pepper and cinnamon. Cover and cook on LOW 3 hours.

2. Stir in apricots, salt and pepper. Cover and cook on LOW 2 to 3 hours, or until lamb is tender and sauce is thickened. Serve lamb over noodles.

Makes 6 servings

Vegetarian Chili

1 tablespoon vegetable oil
1 cup finely chopped onion
1 cup chopped red bell pepper
2 tablespoons minced jalapeño pepper
1 clove garlic, minced
1 can (28 ounces) crushed tomatoes
1 can (14½ ounces) black beans, rinsed and drained
1 can (14 ounces) garbanzo beans, drained
½ cup canned corn
¼ cup tomato paste
1 teaspoon sugar
1 teaspoon ground cumin
1 teaspoon dried basil leaves
1 teaspoon chili powder
¼ teaspoon black pepper
1 cup shredded Cheddar cheese (optional)

1. Heat oil in large nonstick skillet over medium-high heat until hot. Add chopped onion, bell pepper, jalapeño pepper and garlic; cook and stir 5 minutes or until vegetables are tender.

2. Spoon vegetables into slow cooker. Add remaining ingredients, except cheese, to slow cooker; mix well. Cover and cook on LOW 4 to 5 hours. Garnish with cheese, if desired.   *Makes 4 servings*

Vegetarian Chili

Mediterranean Meatball Ratatouille

   2 tablespoons olive oil, divided
   1 pound mild Italian sausage, casings removed
   1 package (8 ounces) sliced mushrooms
   1 small eggplant, diced
   1 zucchini, diced
  ½ cup chopped onion
   1 clove garlic, minced
   1 teaspoon dried oregano leaves
   1 teaspoon salt
  ½ teaspoon black pepper
   1 tablespoon tomato paste
   2 tomatoes, diced
   2 tablespoons chopped fresh basil
   1 teaspoon fresh lemon juice

1. Pour 1 tablespoon olive oil to 5-quart slow cooker. Shape sausage into 1-inch balls. Place half the meatballs in slow cooker. Add half the mushrooms, eggplant and zucchini. Add onion, garlic, ½ teaspoon oregano, ½ teaspoon salt and ¼ teaspoon pepper.

2. Add remaining meatballs, mushrooms, eggplant and zucchini. Add remaining oregano, salt and pepper. Top with remaining olive oil. Cover and cook on LOW 6 to 7 hours.

3. Stir in tomato paste and diced tomatoes. Cover and cook on LOW 15 minutes. Stir in basil and lemon; serve.

Makes 6 (1⅔ cups) servings

*Mediterranean Meatball
Ratatouille*

HEARTY 216 **STEWS**

Black Bean and Sausage Stew

    3 cans (15 ounces each) black beans, drained and
        rinsed
1½ cups chopped onion
1½ cups fat-free reduced-sodium chicken broth
    1 cup sliced celery
    1 cup chopped red bell pepper
    4 cloves garlic, minced
1½ teaspoons dried oregano
    ¾ teaspoon ground coriander
    ½ teaspoon ground cumin
    ¼ teaspoon ground red pepper
    6 ounces cooked turkey sausage, thinly sliced

1. Combine all ingredients in slow cooker, except
sausage. Cover and cook on LOW 6 to 8 hours.

2. Remove about 1½ cups bean mixture from slow
cooker to blender or food processor; purée bean
mixture. Return to slow cooker. Stir in sliced sausage.
Cover and cook on LOW an additional 10 to 15 minutes.

Makes 6 servings

Golden Harvest Stew

   1 pound pork cutlets, cut into 1-inch pieces
   2 tablespoons all-purpose flour, divided
   1 tablespoon vegetable oil
   2 medium Yukon gold potatoes, unpeeled and cut
      into 1-inch cubes
   1 large sweet potato, peeled and cut into 1-inch
      cubes
   1 cup chopped carrots
   1 ear corn, broken into 4 pieces *or* ½ cup canned
      corn
  ½ cup chicken broth
   1 jalapeño pepper, seeded and finely chopped
   1 clove garlic, minced
   1 teaspoon salt
  ¼ teaspoon black pepper
  ¼ teaspoon dried thyme leaves

1. Coat pork pieces with 1 tablespoon flour; set aside. Heat oil in large nonstick skillet over medium-high heat until hot. Brown pork 2 to 3 minutes per side; transfer to 5-quart slow cooker.

2. Add remaining ingredients to slow cooker. Cover and cook on LOW 5 to 6 hours.

3. Combine remaining 1 tablespoon flour and ¼ cup broth from stew in small bowl; stir until smooth. Pour flour mixture into stew; stir. Cover and cook on HIGH 10 minutes.   *Makes 4 (2½-cup) servings*

Chicken and Chili Pepper Stew

- 1 **pound boneless skinless chicken thighs, cut into ½-inch pieces**
- 1 **pound small potatoes, cut lengthwise in halves and then cut crosswise into slices**
- 1 **cup chopped onion**
- 2 **poblano chili peppers, seeded and cut into ½-inch pieces**
- 1 **jalapeño pepper, seeded and finely chopped**
- 3 **cloves garlic, minced**
- 3 **cups fat-free reduced-sodium chicken broth**
- 1 **can (14½ ounces) no-salt-added diced tomatoes**
- 2 **tablespoons chili powder**
- 1 **teaspoon dried oregano leaves**

1. Place chicken, potatoes, onion, poblano peppers, jalapeño pepper and garlic in slow cooker.

2. Stir together broth, tomatoes, chili powder and oregano in large bowl. Pour broth mixture over chicken mixture in slow cooker. Stir. Cover and cook on LOW 8 to 9 hours.   *Makes 6 servings*

Picadillo

1 pound ground beef
1 small onion, chopped
1 clove garlic, minced
1 can (16 ounces) diced tomatoes, undrained
¼ cup golden raisins
1 tablespoon chili powder
1 tablespoon cider vinegar
½ teaspoon ground cumin
½ teaspoon dried oregano leaves
½ teaspoon ground cinnamon
¼ teaspoon red pepper flakes
1 teaspoon salt
¼ cup slivered almonds (optional)

Cook ground beef, onion and garlic in medium nonstick skillet over medium heat until beef is no longer pink; drain. Place mixture in slow cooker. Add tomatoes, raisins, chili powder, vinegar, cumin, oregano, cinnamon and red pepper flakes to slow cooker. Cover and cook on LOW 6 to 7 hours. Stir in salt. Garnish with almonds, if desired.   *Makes 4 servings*

TIP-TOP TATERS

Sweet-Spiced Sweet Potatoes

2 pounds sweet potatoes, peeled and cut into
    ½-inch pieces
¼ **cup dark brown sugar, packed**
  1 **teaspoon ground cinnamon**
½ **teaspoon ground nutmeg**
⅛ **teaspoon salt**
  2 **tablespoons butter, cut into** ⅛-inch pieces
  1 **teaspoon vanilla extract**

Combine all ingredients, except butter and vanilla, in slow cooker; mix well. Cover and cook on LOW 7 hours or cook on HIGH 4 hours. Add butter and vanilla; stir to blend.
Makes 4 servings

Blue Cheese Potatoes

    2 pounds red potatoes, peeled and cut into
        ½-inch pieces
  1¼ cups chopped green onions, divided
    1 teaspoon dried basil leaves
    2 tablespoons olive oil, divided
    ½ teaspoon salt
        Black pepper
    2 ounces crumbled blue cheese

1. Layer potatoes, 1 cup onions, basil, 1 tablespoon oil, salt and pepper in slow cooker. Cover and cook on LOW 7 hours or on HIGH 4 hours.

2. Gently stir in cheese and remaining 1 tablespoon oil. If slow cooker is on low turn to HIGH and cook an additional 5 minutes to allow flavors to blend. Transfer potatoes to serving platter and top with remaining ¼ cup onions.   *Makes 5 servings*

Slow Roasted Potatoes

16 small new potatoes
3 tablespoons butter, cut into ⅛-inch pieces
1 teaspoon paprika
½ teaspoon salt
¼ teaspoon garlic powder
Black pepper to taste

Combine all ingredients in slow cooker; mix well. Cover and cook on LOW 7 hours or on HIGH 4 hours. Remove potatoes with slotted spoon to serving dish; cover to keep warm. Add 1 to 2 tablespoons water to drippings and stir until well blended. Pour mixture over potatoes.

Makes 3 to 4 servings

HELPFUL HINT

New potatoes are freshly dug young potatoes. They may be any variety, but most often are round reds.

Potato-Crab Chowder

   1 cup frozen hash brown potatoes
   1 package (10 ounces) frozen corn
¾ cup finely chopped carrots
   1 teaspoon dried thyme leaves
¾ teaspoon garlic-pepper seasoning
   3 cups fat-fee reduced-sodium chicken broth
½ cup water
   1 cup evaporated milk
   3 tablespoons cornstarch
½ cup sliced green onions
   1 can (6 ounces) crabmeat, drained

1. Place potatoes, corn and carrots in slow cooker. Sprinkle with thyme and garlic-pepper seasoning.

2. Add broth and water. Cover and cook on LOW for 3½ to 4½ hours.

3. Stir together evaporated milk and cornstarch in medium bowl. Stir into slow cooker. Turn temperature to HIGH. Cover and cook 1 hour. Stir in green onions and crabmeat. *Makes 5 servings*

Potato-Crab Chowder

Mediterranean Red Potatoes

2 medium red potatoes, cut in half lengthwise then
    crosswise into pieces
⅔ cup fresh or frozen pearl onions
    Nonstick garlic-flavored cooking spray
¾ teaspoon dried Italian seasoning
¼ teaspoon black pepper
1 small tomato, seeded and chopped
2 ounces feta cheese, crumbled
2 tablespoons chopped black olives

1. Place potatoes and onions in a 1½-quart soufflé dish.
Spray potatoes and onions with cooking spray; toss to
coat. Add Italian seasoning and pepper; mix well. Cover
dish tightly with foil.

2. Make foil handles (see page 276). Place soufflé dish in
slow cooker. Pour hot water to come about 1½ inches
from top of soufflé dish. Cover and cook on LOW 7 to
8 hours.

3. Use foil handles to lift dish from slow cooker. Stir
tomato, feta cheese and olives into potato mixture.

Makes 4 servings

Mediterranean Red
Potatoes

Ham and Potato Casserole

1½ pounds red potatoes, peeled and sliced
8 ounces thinly sliced ham
2 poblano chili peppers, cut into thin strips
2 tablespoons olive oil
1 tablespoon dried oregano leaves
¼ teaspoon salt
1 cup (4 ounces) shredded Monterey Jack cheese
    with or without hot peppers
2 tablespoons finely chopped cilantro leaves

1. Combine all ingredients, except cheese and cilantro, in slow cooker; mix well. Cover and cook on LOW 7 hours or on HIGH 4 hours.

2. Transfer potato mixture to serving dish and sprinkle with cheese and cilantro. Let stand 3 minutes or until cheese melts.   *Makes 6 to 7 servings*

Parmesan Potato Wedges

2 pounds red potatoes, cut into ½-inch wedges
¼ cup finely chopped yellow onion
1½ teaspoons dried oregano leaves
½ teaspoon salt
   Black pepper to taste
2 tablespoons butter, cut into ⅛-inch pieces
¼ cup (1 ounce) grated Parmesan cheese

Layer potatoes, onion, oregano, salt, pepper and butter in slow cooker. Cook on HIGH 4 hours. Transfer potatoes to serving platter and sprinkle with cheese.   *Makes 6 servings*

Rustic Garlic Mashed Potatoes

   2 pounds baking potatoes, unpeeled and cut into
       ½-inch cubes
   ¼ cup water
   2 tablespoons butter, cut in ⅛-inch pieces
   1¼ teaspoons salt
   ½ teaspoon garlic powder
   ¼ teaspoon black pepper
   1 cup milk

Place all ingredients, except milk, in slow cooker; toss to combine. Cover and cook on LOW 7 hours or on HIGH 4 hours. Add milk to slow cooker. Mash potatoes with potato masher or electric mixer until smooth.

Makes 5 servings

HELPFUL HINT

Scrub potatoes with a vegetable brush under warm running water before cooking to remove embedded dirt.

DESSERTS, SNACKS & MORE

Red Pepper Relish

2 large red bell peppers, cut into thin strips
1 small Vidalia or other sweet onion, thinly sliced
3 tablespoons cider vinegar
2 tablespoons brown sugar
1 tablespoon vegetable oil
1 tablespoon honey
¼ teaspoon salt
¼ teaspoon dried thyme leaves
¼ teaspoon red pepper flakes
¼ teaspoon black pepper

Combine all ingredients in slow cooker; mix well. Cover and cook on LOW 4 hours. *Makes 4 servings*

Banana-Rum Custard with Vanilla Wafers

1½ cups milk

3 eggs

½ cup sugar

3 tablespoons dark rum or milk

⅛ teaspoon salt

1 medium banana, sliced ¼-inch thick

15 to 18 vanilla wafers

Sliced strawberries, raspberries or kiwis for garnish (optional)

1. Beat milk, eggs, sugar, rum and salt in medium bowl. Pour into 1-quart casserole. Do not cover.

2. Add rack to 5-quart slow cooker and pour in 1 cup water. Place casserole on rack. Cover and cook on LOW 3½ to 4 hours. Remove casserole from slow cooker. Arrange banana slices and wafers over custard. Garnish with strawberries, raspberries or kiwis, if desired.

Makes 5 servings

Banana-Rum Custard with Vanilla Wafers

Curried Snack Mix

3 tablespoons butter
2 tablespoons brown sugar
1½ teaspoons hot curry powder
¼ teaspoon salt
¼ teaspoon ground cumin
2 cups rice squares cereal
1 cup walnut halves
1 cup dried cranberries

Melt butter in large skillet. Add brown sugar, curry powder, salt and cumin; mix well. Add cereal, walnuts and cranberries and stir to coat. Spoon mixture into slow cooker. Cover and cook on LOW 3 hours. Remove cover; cook an additional 30 minutes.

Makes 16 servings

Cherry Rice Pudding

1½ cups milk
1 cup hot cooked rice
3 eggs, beaten
½ cup sugar
¼ cup dried cherries or cranberries
½ teaspoon almond extract
¼ teaspoon salt

Combine all ingredients in large bowl. Pour mixture into greased 1½-quart casserole. Cover with foil. Add rack to 5-quart slow cooker and pour in 1 cup water. Place casserole on rack. Cover and cook on LOW 4 to 5 hours. Remove casserole from slow cooker. Let stand 15 minutes before serving. *Makes 6 servings*

Spiced Citrus Tea

    4 tea bags
      Peel of 1 orange
    4 cups boiling water
    3 tablespoons honey
    2 cans (6 ounces each) orange-pineapple juice
    3 star anise
    3 cinnamon sticks
      Strawberries, raspberries or kiwis (optional)

1. Place tea bags and orange peel in slow cooker. Pour in boiling water. Cover and let steep 10 minutes. Discard tea bags and orange peel.

2. Add remaining ingredients to slow cooker. Cover and cook on LOW 3 hours. Garnish with strawberries, raspberries or kiwis, if desired.   *Makes 6 servings*

HELPFUL HINT

Star anise can be found in Asian markets, gourmet shops and in some larger supermarkets.

Chocolate Croissant Pudding

1½ cups milk
3 eggs
½ cup sugar
¼ cup unsweetened cocoa powder
½ teaspoon vanilla
¼ teaspoon salt
2 plain croissants, cut into 1-inch pieces.
½ cup chocolate chips
¾ cup whipped cream (optional)

1. Beat milk, eggs, sugar, cocoa, vanilla and salt in medium bowl.

2. Grease a 1-quart casserole. Layer half the croissants, chocolate chips and half the egg mixture in casserole. Repeat layers with remaining croissants and egg mixture.

3. Add rack to 5-quart slow cooker and pour in 1 cup water. Place casserole on rack. Cover and cook on LOW 3 to 4 hours. Remove casserole from slow cooker. Top each serving with 2 tablespoons whipped cream, if desired.   *Makes 6 servings*

*Chocolate Croissant
Pudding*

Triple Delicious Hot Chocolate

⅓ cup sugar
¼ cup unsweetened cocoa powder
¼ teaspoon salt
3 cups milk, divided
¾ teaspoon vanilla extract
1 cup heavy cream
1 square (1 ounce) bittersweet chocolate
1 square (1 ounce) white chocolate
¾ cup whipped cream
6 teaspoons mini chocolate chips *or* shaved
    bittersweet chocolate

1. Combine sugar, cocoa, salt and ½ cup milk in medium bowl. Beat until smooth. Pour into slow cooker. Add remaining milk and vanilla. Cover and cook on LOW 2 hours.

2. Add cream. Cover and cook on LOW 10 minutes. Stir in bittersweet and white chocolates.

3. Pour hot chocolate into 6 coffee cups. Top each with 2 tablespoons whipped cream and 1 teaspoon chocolate chips.   *Makes 6 servings*

My Favorites

Favorite recipe: _____

Favorite recipe from: _____

Ingredients: _____

_____

_____

_____

_____

_____

Method: _____

_____

_____

_____

_____

_____

_____

_____

_____

_____

_____

My Favorite Recipes

Favorite recipe: _____

Favorite recipe from: _____

Ingredients: _____

_____

_____

_____

_____

_____

Method: _____

_____

_____

_____

_____

_____

_____

_____

_____

_____

_____

My Favorite Recipes

Favorite recipe: _____

Favorite recipe from: _____

Ingredients: _____

_____

_____

_____

_____

_____

Method: _____

_____

_____

_____

_____

_____

_____

_____

_____

_____

_____

My Favorite Recipes

Favorite recipe: _____

Favorite recipe from: _____

Ingredients: _____

_____

_____

_____

_____

_____

Method: _____

_____

_____

_____

_____

_____

_____

_____

_____

_____

_____

_____

My Favorite Recipes

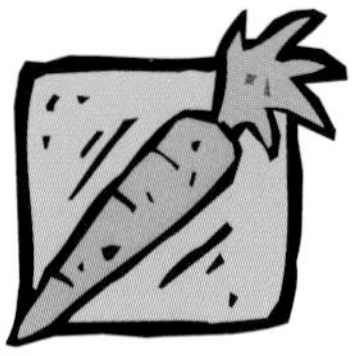

Favorite recipe: ______________________________

Favorite recipe from: ______________________________

Ingredients: ______________________________

____

____

____

____

____

Method: ______________________________

____

____

____

____

____

____

____

____

____

____

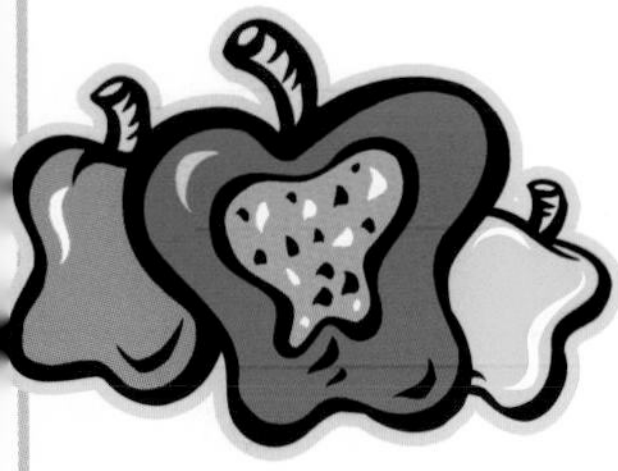

____

____

My Favorite Recipes

Favorite recipe: _____

Favorite recipe from: _____

Ingredients: _____

_____

_____

_____

_____

_____

Method: _____

_____

_____

_____

_____

_____

_____

_____

_____

_____

_____

_____

_____

Favorite recipe: _____

Favorite recipe from: _____

Ingredients: _____

_____

_____

_____

_____

_____

Method: _____

_____

_____

_____

_____

_____

_____

_____

_____

_____

_____

_____

My Favorite Recipes

Favorite recipe: _____

Favorite recipe from: _____

Ingredients: _____

_____

_____

_____

_____

_____

Method: _____

_____

_____

_____

_____

_____

_____

_____

_____

_____

_____

_____

_____

248

My Favorite Recipes

Favorite recipe: _____

Favorite recipe from: _____

Ingredients: _____

_____

_____

_____

_____

_____

Method: _____

_____

_____

_____

_____

_____

_____

_____

_____

_____

_____

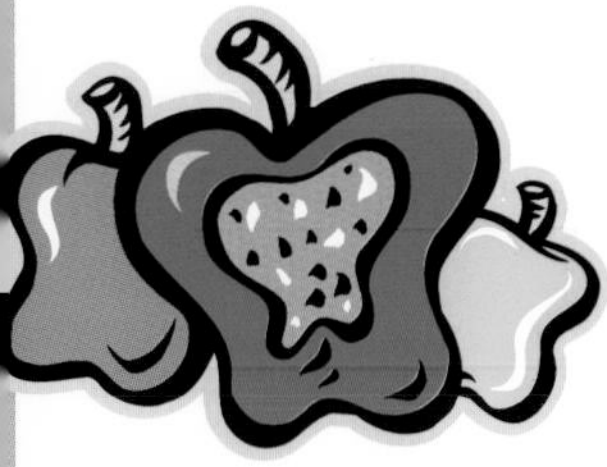

_____

My Favorite Recipes

Favorite recipe: _____

Favorite recipe from: _____

Ingredients: _____

_____

_____

_____

_____

_____

Method: _____

_____

_____

_____

_____

_____

_____

_____

_____

_____

_____

_____

My Favorite Recipes

Favorite recipe: _____

Favorite recipe from: _____

Ingredients: _____

_____

_____

_____

_____

_____

Method: _____

_____

_____

_____

_____

_____

_____

_____

_____

_____

_____

My Favorite Recipes

Favorite recipe: _____

Favorite recipe from: _____

Ingredients: _____

_____

_____

_____

_____

_____

Method: _____

_____

_____

_____

_____

_____

_____

_____

_____

_____

_____

_____

My Favorite Recipes

Favorite recipe: _____

Favorite recipe from: _____

Ingredients: _____

_____

_____

_____

_____

_____

Method: _____

_____

_____

_____

_____

_____

_____

_____

_____

_____

My Favorite Recipes

Favorite recipe: _____

Favorite recipe from: _____

Ingredients: _____

_____

_____

_____

_____

_____

Method: _____

_____

_____

_____

_____

_____

_____

_____

_____

_____

_____

_____

My Favorite Recipes

Favorite recipe: _____

Favorite recipe from: _____

Ingredients: _____

_____

_____

_____

_____

_____

Method: _____

_____

_____

_____

_____

_____

_____

_____

_____

_____

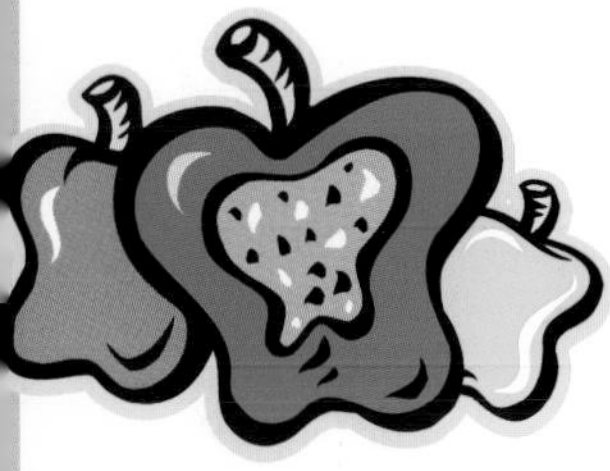

My Favorite Recipes

Favorite recipe: _____

Favorite recipe from: _____

Ingredients: _____

_____

_____

_____

_____

_____

Method: _____

_____

_____

_____

_____

_____

_____

_____

_____

_____

_____

My Favorite Recipes

Favorite recipe: _____

Favorite recipe from: _____

Ingredients: _____

_____

_____

_____

_____

_____

Method: _____

_____

_____

_____

_____

_____

_____

_____

_____

_____

_____

_____

257

My Favorite Recipes

Favorite recipe: _____

Favorite recipe from: _____

Ingredients: _____

_____

_____

_____

_____

_____

Method: _____

_____

_____

_____

_____

_____

_____

_____

_____

_____

_____

My Favorite Recipes

Favorite recipe: _____

Favorite recipe from: _____

Ingredients: _____

_____

_____

_____

_____

_____

Method: _____

_____

_____

_____

_____

_____

_____

_____

_____

_____

My Favorite Recipes

Favorite recipe: _____

Favorite recipe from: _____

Ingredients: _____

_____

_____

_____

_____

_____

Method: _____

_____

_____

_____

_____

_____

_____

_____

_____

_____

_____

_____

My Favorite Recipes

Favorite recipe: _____

Favorite recipe from: _____

_____

Ingredients: _____

_____

_____

_____

_____

Method: _____

_____

_____

_____

_____

_____

_____

_____

_____

_____

_____

_____

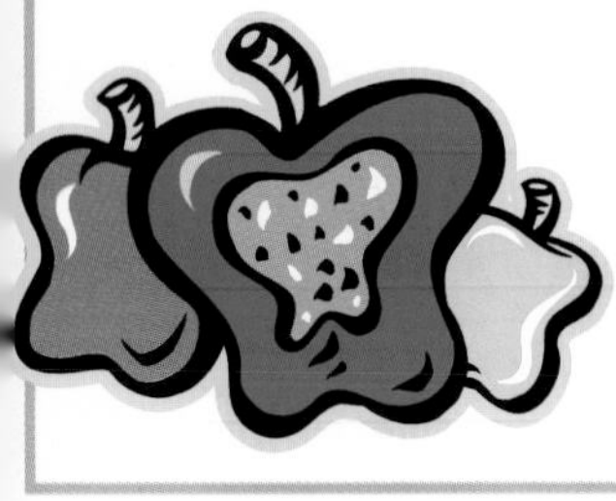

My Favorite Weeknight Meals

Favorite recipe: _____

Favorite recipe from: _____
_____

Ingredients: _____
_____
_____
_____
_____

Method: _____
_____
_____
_____
_____
_____
_____
_____
_____
_____
_____
_____
_____

My Favorite Weeknight Meals

Favorite recipe: _____

Favorite recipe from: _____
_____

Ingredients: _____
_____
_____
_____
_____

Method: _____
_____
_____
_____
_____
_____
_____
_____
_____
_____
_____
_____

My Favorite Dinner Party

Date: _____

Occasion: _____
_____

Guests: _____
_____
_____
_____
_____

Menu: _____
_____
_____
_____
_____
_____
_____
_____
_____
_____
_____

My Favorite Dinner Party

Date: _____

Occasion: _____
_____

Guests: _____
_____
_____
_____
_____

Menu: _____
_____
_____
_____
_____
_____
_____
_____
_____
_____
_____

My Favorite Pot-Luck Recipes

Favorite recipe: _____

Favorite recipe from: _____

_____

Ingredients: _____

_____

_____

_____

_____

Method: _____

_____

_____

_____

_____

_____

_____

_____

_____

_____

_____

_____

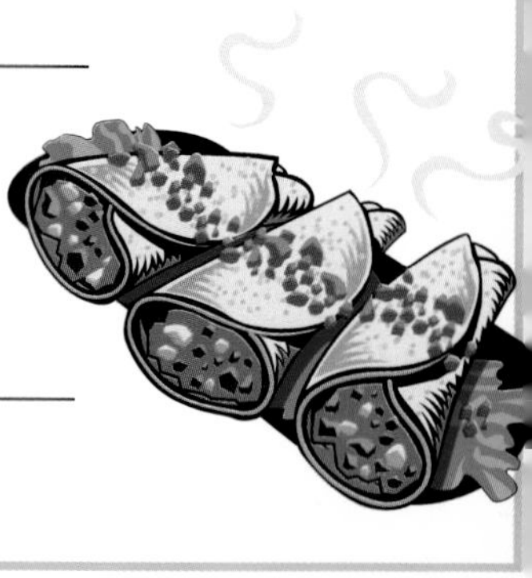

My Favorite Pot-Luck Recipes

Favorite recipe: _____

Favorite recipe from: _____

_____

Ingredients: _____

_____

_____

_____

_____

Method: _____

_____

_____

_____

_____

_____

_____

_____

_____

_____

My Favorite Pot-Luck Recipes

Favorite recipe: _____

Favorite recipe from: _____

_____

Ingredients: _____

_____

_____

_____

_____

Method: _____

_____

_____

_____

_____

_____

_____

_____

_____

_____

_____

_____

_____

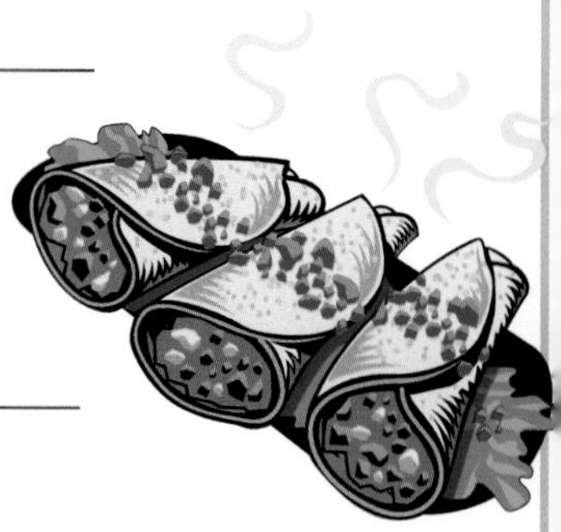

My Favorite Pot-Luck Recipes

Favorite recipe: _____

Favorite recipe from: _____

_____

Ingredients: _____

_____

_____

_____

_____

Method: _____

_____

_____

_____

_____

_____

_____

_____

_____

_____

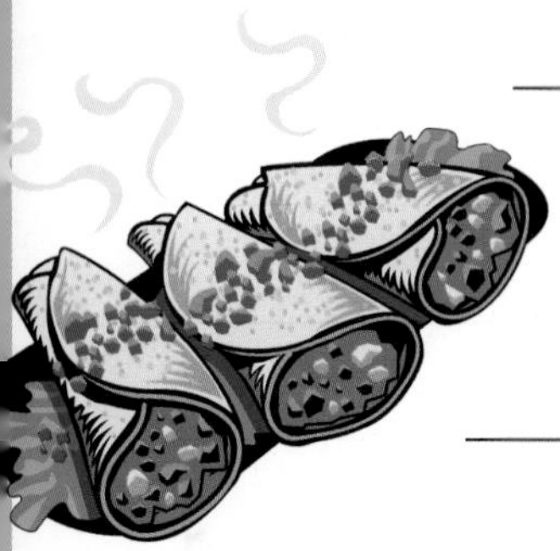

My Favorite Pot-Luck Recipes

Favorite recipe: _____

Favorite recipe from: _____

_____

Ingredients: _____

_____

_____

_____

_____

Method: _____

_____

_____

_____

_____

_____

_____

_____

_____

_____

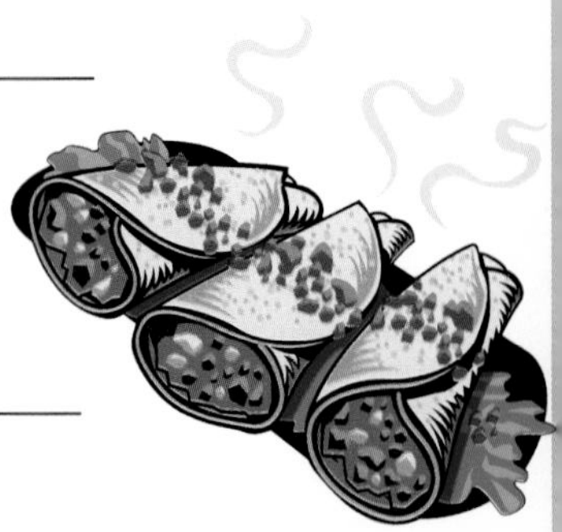

My Favorite Friends

Friend: _____

Favorite foods: _____

_____

_____

_____

_____

_____

Don't serve: _____

_____

_____

_____

_____

_____

_____

_____

_____

_____

_____

_____

My Favorite Friends

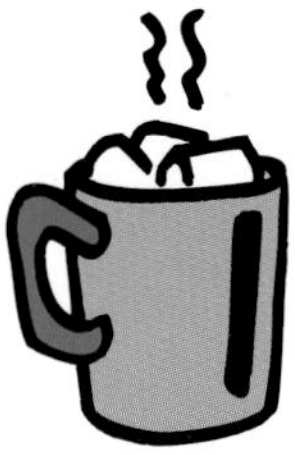

Friend: ______________________________

Favorite foods: ______________________________

Don't serve: ______________________________

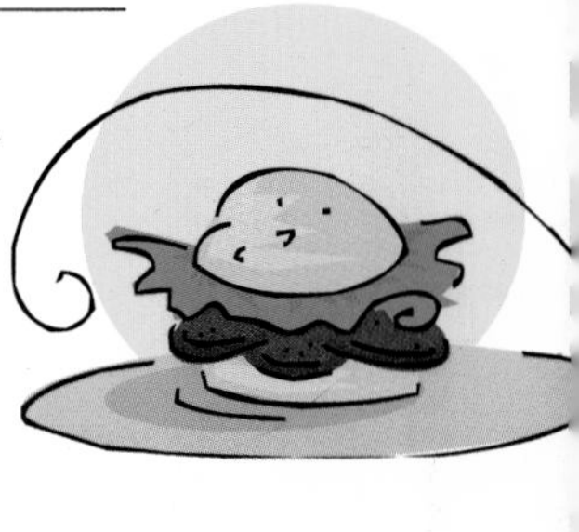

The Basics

- Slow cookers were introduced in the 1970's, found new popularity in the 1990's and are guaranteed to continue there growth into the new millennium.

- As with conventional cooking recipes, slow cooker recipe time ranges are provided to account for variables such as temperature of ingredients before cooking, how full the slow cooker is and even altitude. Once you become familiar with your slow cooker you'll have a good idea which end of the range to use.

- Manufacturers recommend that slow cookers should be one-half to three-quarters full for best results.

- Keep a lid on it! The slow cooker can take as long as twenty minutes to regain the heat lost when the cover is removed. If the recipe calls for stirring or checking the dish near the end of the cooking time, replace the lid as quickly as you can.

- Save money and gain flavor by choosing tougher inexpensive cuts of meat for use with the slow cooker recipes. The long cooking times help break down the toughness of the meat.

- To clean your slow cooker, follow the manufacturer's instructions. To make cleanup even easier, spray with nonstick cooking spray before adding food.

- Always taste the finished dish before serving and adjust seasonings to your preference. Consider adding a dash of any of the following: salt, pepper, seasoned salt, seasoned herb blends, lemon juice, soy sauce, Worcestershire sauce, flavored vinegar, freshly ground pepper or minced fresh herbs.

The Benefits

- There is no need for constant attention or stirring.

- You never have to worry about burning or overcooking.

- Your sink will be free from pots and pans to scrub at the end of a long day.

- It is the perfect helper for parties and buffets.

- You kitchen will stay cool since it keeps your oven turned off.

- Even though the slow cooker is on for hours, it saves you energy. When cooking on the low setting, it uses less energy than most light bulbs.

TIPS & TECHNIQUES

Adapting Recipes

If you'd like to adapt your own favorite recipe to a slow cooker, you'll need to follow a few guidelines. First, try to find a similar recipe in this publication or your manufacturer's guide. Note the cooking times, liquid, quantity and size of meat and vegetable pieces. Because the slow cooker captures moisture, you will want to reduce the amount of liquid, often by as much as half. Add dairy products toward the end of the cooking time so they don't curdle.

Slow Cooker Tips

Selecting the Right Meat

A good tip to keep in mind while shopping is that you can, and in fact should, use tougher, inexpensive cuts of meat. Top-quality cuts, such as loin chops or filet mignon, fall apart during the long cooking periods. Keep those for roasting, broiling or grilling and save money when you use your slow cooker. You will be amazed to find even the toughest cuts come out fork-tender and flavorful.

Reducing Fat

The slow cooker can help you make meals lower in fat because you won't be cooking in fat as you do when you stir-fry and sauté. And tougher cuts of meat have less fat than prime cuts.

If you do use fatty cuts, such as ribs, consider browning them first on top of the range to cook off excess fat.

Chicken skin tends to shrivel and curl in the slow cooker; therefore, most recipes call for skinless chicken. If you use skin-on pieces, brown them before adding them to the slow cooker. If you would rather remove the skin, use the following technique: freeze chicken until firm but not hard. (Do not freeze thawed chicken.) Grasp chicken with clean kitchen towel or paper towel and pull away from meat; discard skin. When finished skinning chicken, launder towel before using again.

You can easily remove most of the fat from accumulated juices, soups and canned broths. The simplest way is to refrigerate the liquid for several hours or overnight. The fat will congeal and float to the top for easy removal. If you plan to use the liquid right away, ladle it into a bowl or measuring cup. Let it stand about 5 minutes so the fat can rise to the surface. Skim with a large spoon. You can also lightly pull a sheet of clean paper towel over the surface, letting the grease be absorbed. To degrease canned broth, refrigerate the unopened can. Simply spoon the congealed fat off the surface after opening the can.

Cutting Your Vegetables

Vegetables often take longer to cook than meats. Cut the vegetables into small, thin pieces and place them on the bottom or near the sides of the slow cooker. Pay careful attention to the recipe instructions in order to cut vegetables to the proper size.

Foil to the Rescue

To easily lift a dish or a meatloaf out of the slow cooker, make foil handles according to the following directions.

Tear off three 18×3-inch strips of heavy-duty foil. Crisscross the strips so they resemble the spokes of a wheel. Place your dish or food in center of the strips.

Pull the foil strips up and over and place into the slow cooker. Leave them in while you cook so you can easily lift the item out again when ready.

Food Safety Tips

Your best weapon against food contamination is organization. A clean and organized kitchen is a happy kitchen.

Read the entire recipe before you begin to be sure you have all the necessary ingredients and utensils required.

It is a good idea to have two cutting boards on hand. Use one for cutting raw meat, poultry and fish and the other for cutting fresh fruits, vegetables and other foods. Always wash cutting boards and utensils with hot soapy water after each use.

If you do any advance preparation, such as trimming meat or cutting vegetables, refrigerate the food until you're ready to start cooking. Store food in resealable plastic food storage bags. To avoid cross contamination, always place raw meat, poultry and fish on the lowest shelf in the refrigerator. Place fruits and vegetables on higher shelves or in a crisper drawer.

Once your dish is cooked, don't keep it in the slow cooker too long. Foods need to be kept cooler than 40°F or hotter than 140°F to avoid the growth of harmful bacteria. Remove food to a clean container, cover and refrigerate as soon as possible. Do not reheat leftovers in the slow cooker. Use a microwave oven, the range-top or the oven for reheating.

General Substitutions

If you don't have:	**Use:**
1 cup buttermilk	1 tablespoon lemon juice or vinegar plus milk to equal 1 cup (stir; let stand 5 minutes)
1 tablespoon cornstarch	2 tablespoons all-purpose flour or 2 teaspoons arrowroot
1 whole egg	2 egg yolks plus 1 teaspoon cold water
1 teaspoon vinegar	2 teaspoons lemon juice
1 cup whole milk	1 cup skim milk plus 2 tablespoons melted butter
1 cup sour cream	1 cup plain yogurt

Dash = Less than ⅛ teaspoon

½ tablespoon = 1½ teaspoons

1 tablespoon = 3 teaspoons

⅛ cup = 2 tablespoons

¼ cup = 4 tablespoons

⅓ cup = 5 tablespoons plus 1 teaspoon

½ cup = 8 tablespoons

¾ cup = 12 tablespoons

1 cup = 16 tablespoons

½ pint = 1 cup or 8 fluid ounces

1 pint = 2 cups or 16 fluid ounces

1 quart = 4 cups or 2 pints or 32 fluid ounces

1 gallon = 16 cups or 4 quarts or 128 fluid ounces

1 pound = 16 ounces

Metric Conversion Chart

VOLUME MEASUREMENTS (dry)

$1/8$ teaspoon = 0.5 mL
$1/4$ teaspoon = 1 mL
$1/2$ teaspoon = 2 mL
$3/4$ teaspoon = 4 mL
1 teaspoon = 5 mL
1 tablespoon = 15 mL
2 tablespoons = 30 mL
$1/4$ cup = 60 mL
$1/3$ cup = 75 mL
$1/2$ cup = 125 mL
$2/3$ cup = 150 mL
$3/4$ cup = 175 mL
1 cup = 250 mL
2 cups = 1 pint = 500 mL
3 cups = 750 mL
4 cups = 1 quart = 1 L

VOLUME MEASUREMENTS (fluid)

1 fluid ounce (2 tablespoons) = 30 mL
4 fluid ounces ($1/2$ cup) = 125 mL
8 fluid ounces (1 cup) = 250 mL
12 fluid ounces ($1 1/2$ cups) = 375 mL
16 fluid ounces (2 cups) = 500 mL

WEIGHTS (mass)

$1/2$ ounce = 15 g
1 ounce = 30 g
3 ounces = 90 g
4 ounces = 120 g
8 ounces = 225 g
10 ounces = 285 g
12 ounces = 360 g
16 ounces = 1 pound = 450 g

DIMENSIONS

$1/16$ inch = 2 mm
$1/8$ inch = 3 mm
$1/4$ inch = 6 mm
$1/2$ inch = 1.5 cm
$3/4$ inch = 2 cm
1 inch = 2.5 cm

OVEN TEMPERATURES

250°F = 120°C
275°F = 140°C
300°F = 150°C
325°F = 160°C
350°F = 180°C
375°F = 190°C
400°F = 200°C
425°F = 220°C
450°F = 230°C

BAKING PAN SIZES

Utensil	Size in Inches/Quarts	Metric Volume	Size in Centimeters
Baking or Cake Pan (square or rectangular)	$8 \times 8 \times 2$	2 L	$20 \times 20 \times 5$
	$9 \times 9 \times 2$	2.5 L	$23 \times 23 \times 5$
	$12 \times 8 \times 2$	3 L	$30 \times 20 \times 5$
	$13 \times 9 \times 2$	3.5 L	$33 \times 23 \times 5$
Loaf Pan	$8 \times 4 \times 3$	1.5 L	$20 \times 10 \times 7$
	$9 \times 5 \times 3$	2 L	$23 \times 13 \times 7$
Round Layer Cake Pan	$8 \times 1 1/2$	1.2 L	20×4
	$9 \times 1 1/2$	1.5 L	23×4
Pie Plate	$8 \times 1 1/4$	750 mL	20×3
	$9 \times 1 1/4$	1 L	23×3
Baking Dish or Casserole	1 quart	1 L	—
	$1 1/2$ quart	1.5 L	—
	2 quart	2 L	—

Acknowledgments

**The publisher would like to thank
the companies and organizations listed
below for the use of their recipes and
photographs in this publication.**

A.1.® Steak Sauce

Butterball® Turkey Company

Campbell Soup Company

Del Monte Corporation

Lawry's® Foods, Inc.

Reckitt Benckiser

Index

Index

Index

Index

Index

Index